SAY HELLO FIRST

A Therapist's Guide to
Building Confidence
and
Finally Making Friends

---

by BIANCA CUMMINGS

Say Hello First
© 2025 Bianca Cummings

All rights reserved. No part of this publication may be reproduced, stored in a retrieval system, or transmitted in any form or by any means—electronic, mechanical, photocopying, recording, or otherwise—without the prior written permission of the author, except in the case of brief quotations used in critical articles or reviews.

This is a work of nonfiction. Some names and identifying details have been changed to protect the privacy of individuals. Only the author's personal stories are factual and true to her lived experiences. All other stories, case studies, and examples are illustrative in nature and are intended solely to support the concepts presented in this book.

Disclaimer:
This book is for informational and educational purposes only. It is not intended as a substitute for professional advice, diagnosis, or treatment. Always seek the guidance of a qualified mental health provider or medical professional with any questions you may have regarding a physical, emotional, or psychological condition. The author and publisher are not responsible for any actions taken based on the content of this book.

For permissions, bulk orders, or speaking inquiries, visit:
www.sayhellofirst.com

Published by Say Hello First Books
An imprint of Bianca Cummings Counseling PLLC

ISBN (Hardcover): 979-8-9991364-1-1
ISBN (Paperback): 979-8-9991364-0-4
ISBN (eBook): 979-8-9991364-2-8

First Edition
Published August 2025

Printed in the United States of America

10 9 8 7 6 5 4 3 2 1

Dedication

To Stephanie—your bright smile, bold spirit, and kind heart light up every room. You are, and have always been, pure sunshine.

To Paul—for being my anchor through this journey, steady and patient, with a heart as deep as the sea.

To Nick, Vinny, and Ginger—your paw prints remain forever on my heart.

And to my clients—this book is for you. Thank you for your trust, your courage, and the inspiration behind every page.

TABLE OF CONTENTS

Introduction   1

PART 1
FROM LONELY TO CONNECTED
LONELINESS AND THE SCIENCE OF CONNECTION

Chapter 1
The Truth About Loneliness   9

Chapter 2
The Power of Balanced Energy to Change Your Life   27

Chapter 3
Interpersonal Synchrony   43

Chapter 4
The Science of Connection and Happiness   57

PART 2
BUILDING INTERNAL CONFIDENCE
HOW YOU EXPERIENCE THE WORLD

Chapter 5
The Confidence to Be You   81

Chapter 6
Stop Being So Hard on Yourself   99

Chapter 7
Social Anxiety: A Way Out   119

Chapter 8
You're More Likable Than You Think   141

PART 3
BUILDING EXTERNAL CONFIDENCE
HOW THE WORLD EXPERIENCES YOU

Chapter 9

The Power of Body Language and Presence   171

Chapter 10

How You Make Them Feel Matters Most   199

Chapter 11

Say Hello First: The Art of Starting a Conversation   223

Chapter 12

Navigating Friendship: Where to Meet, How to Connect   245

Bonus Chapter

Need a Friend? Get a Dog   267

PART 4
RESOURCES AND REFERENCES

Recommended Resources   295

Bibliography   301

Take the Next Brave Step   317

Let's Stay in Touch   318

About the Author   319

What Readers Are Saying

*"A must-read for anyone
who wants to belong.
I would recommend this
to my clients."*
— Amanda T., LPC

*"Heartfelt, beautifully written,
deeply relatable,
and full of useful tools
I'll carry with me."*
— Joyce C.

Introduction

Your Key to Connection

*"We may not have it all together,
but together we have it all."*
— *Unknown*

Think back to high school. We learned how to write five-paragraph essays, label the parts of a cell, and solve for X—but no one taught us how to make friends. Where was the class on how to confidently connect with others? Where was the lesson on being yourself without second-guessing every word? The crash course on what to do when you feel left out, like you're the only one missing some unspoken social rulebook?

Wouldn't it have been life-changing to learn how to develop that effortless likability, that magnetic presence that makes people feel comfortable and drawn to you? How to navigate conversations without awkward pauses or overthinking? How to read body language like an FBI profiler while fine-tuning your own to project confidence and approachability? Where to actually meet new people and turn them into real friends?

If you've ever wished for a roadmap to social confidence: a simple, clear guide on how to connect with people in a way that feels natural, effortless, and fun, you're in the right place.

Because the truth is, making friends and feeling like you belong isn't about luck or natural charm. It's a skill that anyone can learn.

And that's exactly what this book is here to help you do.

Social connections are at the root of everything. You want to feel confident? You need people who lift you up. You want to handle life's curveballs better? Having a support system makes all the difference. You want to find your purpose? That's way easier when you're not doing life solo.

Bottom line: *Connection is the foundation, not the cherry on top.*

Why Making Friends Feels So Hard

You don't need me to tell you that making friends as an adult (or teenager) is harder than anyone prepared us for.

Sure, people say, *"Just put yourself out there!"* Or, *"Just be yourself!"* But no one ever explains **how** to do that when you're already feeling awkward, anxious, or out of place.

Maybe you've tried. You've made small talk, said yes to invitations, and even pushed past your comfort zone. But still, something feels off. The friendships don't stick, the connections feel surface-level, and deep down, you're wondering:

Is it just me?

Here's the good news: **It's not just you, and it's not your fault.**

The way we build friendships has changed, but our brains haven't caught up yet. The problem isn't you. It's the hidden forces that shape the way we connect (or struggle to). And once you understand them, making friends won't just feel easier, it'll feel natural. Let's look at what might really be holding you back, not your words, but the energy behind them.

Balanced Energy: Your Key to Genuine Connection

At the heart of this book is a simple but powerful idea: **your energy—how you carry yourself, how you feel, and what you project—shapes every relationship in your life.**

Before you even say a word, your **energy and presence** communicate something to the people around you. Confidence, warmth, anxiety, self-doubt—people can sense it all, just like you can sense it in others.

I first realized this while watching *The Dog Whisperer* with Cesar Millan. Dogs have an incredible ability to sense and respond to the energy we project. Cesar Millan says, "When a dog is balanced, you are going to enjoy a true friend." When we are balanced, calm, present, and grounded, dogs naturally mirror that energy. They trust us, relax, and become the steady companions we need.

If you've ever seen the show, you know that the problem is almost never the dog; it's the human. Their anxiety, fear, or frustration is reflected back to them by their pet. When the person finds *inner balance*, the dog responds with trust.

And that's when it hit me:

What if human relationships work the same way?

What if the energy you bring into a room—your confidence, your anxiety, your authenticity—shapes every social interaction you have? And what if learning to balance that energy is the key to real, lasting friendships?

The truth is, people respond to how you show up. When you feel good in your own skin, you naturally put others at ease. When you project confidence (even if you don't feel it 100% yet), people gravitate toward you.

By shifting your emotional energy, even slightly, you can make friendships feel effortless instead of awkward.

And the best part? This has nothing to do with changing your personality.

One of the biggest myths about confidence is that you have to become someone you're not. You don't.

This book isn't about pretending to be more outgoing if you're naturally reserved. It's not about masking who you are or forcing yourself to fit in. It's about helping you reconnect with the version of yourself that feels calm, clear, and confident around others.

Because here's the truth: everyone needs connection.

It doesn't matter whether you're an introvert, extrovert, or somewhere in between; human connection is essential for your mental health, well-being, and happiness.

What varies isn't whether we need connection, it's how we create it.

- Introverts might prefer one-on-one conversations or deeper, quieter friendships.
- Extroverts might thrive in larger, social spaces with frequent interaction.
- Ambiverts (somewhere in the middle) might need a balance of people time and alone time.

No matter where you fall on the spectrum, connection is a skill, one you can develop in a way that feels true to you. And that's what this book is here to help you do.

You Don't Have to Do This Alone

If you're holding this book, it means you're ready for something to shift. You're tired of that invisible weight of loneliness, and you're ready for a real, meaningful connection.

That takes courage.

Give yourself credit, you're here, and that matters.

I know firsthand how isolating loneliness can feel. It's like a shadow that follows you around even in a crowded room. I've been there. And as a therapist with a geek-level love for psychology and neuroscience, I've spent years figuring out how to help people just like you turn that feeling around.

This book is your roadmap to belonging—not by becoming someone you're not, but by tapping into the confidence and connection that are already inside you.

Let's be real, this isn't some book of fake tricks or forced small talk. It's about changing how you think about friendship, confidence, and connection so that socializing stops feeling like a performance and starts feeling natural.

Here's a quick look at what's ahead:

- **Part 1: Understanding Loneliness and the Science of Connection.** Why loneliness feels so heavy—and how your brain and emotions shape the way you connect.
- **Part 2: Building Internal Confidence—How You Experience the World.** Learn to shift your mindset, quiet self-doubt, and show up as your best self.
- **Part 3: Building External Confidence—How the World Experiences You.** Practical strategies to project warmth, deepen conversations, and find your people.
- **Part 4: Resources and References—Keep the Connection Going.** The books, studies, and tools that inspired this book and that I still turn to for insight and connection. I hope they'll do the same for you.

This journey doesn't end with the last page. If you're ready to keep growing, start there. You've got this and you're not doing it alone.

Let's Get Started

Whether you're looking for new friends or want to feel more at ease socially, **you belong here**.

And together, we're going to prove it.

Part 1

From Lonely to Connected

Loneliness and

The Science of Connection

**Ready to break free from isolation?
Let's get started right now!**

Chapter 1

The Truth About Loneliness

"Loneliness and the feeling of being unwanted is the most terrible poverty."
— Mother Teresa

I'll never forget how lonely I felt during one of the most amazing times of my life, becoming a first-time mom. A year before my daughter was born, my husband got a promotion, and we decided to pack up our lives in Atlanta and move to Pennsylvania for his new job. It felt like a fresh start, but wow, was it overwhelming. We left behind everything—our friends, family, and the entire support system we'd built over the years.

At least we had our two dogs, Nick, a sweet, stoic 3-year-old chow-shepherd mix, and Vinny, our goofy 1½-year-old golden retriever mix, who was basically the dog version of a stand-up comedian. They weren't just pets, they were family. They came along for the ride, and little did I know, they'd become my lifeline in ways I couldn't yet see.

At first, the move felt exciting: a new city, new opportunities. But the thrill wore off fast. It didn't take long for me to feel like

I'd been plucked out of everything familiar and tossed into the middle of nowhere.

I missed my people.

I missed my routine.

You know who didn't miss a beat? Nick and Vinny. They adjusted like champs.

Nick, ever the loyal protector, would sit quietly beside me when I felt homesick, his big, soulful eyes silently saying, *I've got you.* And Vinny? He was pure comic relief, bounding through the house, chasing his tail like he was auditioning for a sitcom, always managing to make me laugh when I needed it most.

Then, in March of 2003, we got the news: we were pregnant with our first baby. The excitement hit fast, and so did the panic. I was between jobs, which added a fresh layer of stress. And to make things even more chaotic, we decided to move again. This time just a few miles away, into our very first house, a fixer-upper in Delaware that looked like a construction zone.

My husband was working long hours, and when he wasn't at the office, he was tearing up floors and painting walls, trying to get the place baby-ready. Meanwhile, I was walking around a new neighborhood, eight months pregnant, with no friends and no clue what I was doing.

That's when Nick and Vinny really showed up for me. Those two kept me grounded when everything else felt upside down. Our daily walks became a ritual, a quiet slice of normal in the middle of chaos. Nick stayed close by, steady and calm. Vinny pranced ahead, sniffing every mailbox like it held a golden ticket.

It wasn't just about fresh air. It was about *belonging* to something, to someone, to a rhythm that reminded me I wasn't totally alone.

Stephanie was born on December 1, 2003, and those first few weeks were the usual whirlwind of new-mom chaos. I barely had time to think between family visits, late-night feedings, and the sheer awe of holding this tiny human in my arms.

Nick and Vinny were curious but gentle around her, tiptoeing over to sniff her tiny toes like she was some kind of alien life form. But by mid-January, reality set in.

The visitors stopped.

My husband's job kept him traveling.

The phone calls slowed.

And suddenly, I found myself alone in the house with a newborn. It was 2004, before Facebook mom groups, before Instagram stories. If you didn't already have a circle of mom friends, you were on your own. And with winter in full force, I was stuck inside most days, 24/7.

Bring on the loneliness.

Thank goodness for Nick and Vinny. They were my constant companions, quietly reliable, endlessly comforting. Vinny kept me laughing with his antics, like the time he "helped" me fold laundry and ended up dragging one of my socks around like it was his greatest treasure. And Nick? He was my shadow, steady, silent, and always by my side, offering a kind of emotional gravity that made the overwhelm feel manageable.

Looking back now, I realize how much they carried me through those first two years of motherhood. They weren't just dogs; they were my support system, my grounding force, my chosen family.

Even in my loneliest moments, they reminded me that love and connection don't have to be loud or complicated. Sometimes it's just a wagging tail, a quiet sigh, or a shared moment on the couch that reminds you you're not alone.

When we moved back to Georgia in October of 2005, it felt like I was finally coming up for air. Back among friends and family, I began to reconnect with others and with myself.

Widespread Nature of Loneliness

If there's one thing I want you to know, it's this: you're not alone in feeling lonely. Loneliness affects millions of people, and it doesn't discriminate against anyone. Whether you're young or old, thriving or struggling, surrounded by people or physically alone, loneliness has a way of sneaking in when you least expect it.

Imagine you're seven years old, standing on stage for your school's big end-of-year performance. You're scanning the audience for a familiar face, your parents, your family, someone. But all you see are strangers. Your stomach drops. You're suddenly aware of the spotlight, the silence, the fact that you're completely alone, even in a room full of people.

That's the thing about loneliness. It's not about how many people are around. It's about how seen and connected you feel. And when that connection's missing? It's like being that kid on stage, wondering if anyone showed up for you.

Modern life only amplifies the problem. Sure, we're more "connected" than ever, but it's often surface-level. We scroll through social media and see everyone's highlight reel—vacations, promotions, baby announcements—while quietly battling our own moments of disconnection.

> **LONELINESS IN AMERICA**
> - 50% of Americans report feeling lonely.
> - 61% of young adults (ages 18-25) experience severe loneliness.
> - 1 in 5 adults say they often or always feel socially isolated.

It's easy to feel like everyone else has it all together while you're barely holding it down. You can be in a full group chat and still feel completely unseen. Loneliness looks different for everyone. It might be:

- A college student, surrounded by classmates, missing their childhood best friend
- A parent who's never alone, but feels emotionally invisible
- A recently divorced adult navigating life without their usual social rhythm
- An empty-nester feeling the unexpected echo of a quiet home
- A 70-something widow, facing the compounded loss of a partner, siblings, and lifelong friends
- A high-achieving professional with a full calendar but no one to share the real stuff with

Loneliness doesn't care about your résumé or your relationship status. It's not a reflection of your worth. It's a signal that something needs care.

And the good news?

It's not permanent.

You have the power to change it.

> *"Loneliness isn't just a feeling—it's a signal. It's your mind and body telling you that something needs to change."*
>
> — Dr. Vivek Murthy, Together,
> U.S. Surgeon General

Mr. Garcia's Story

Mr. Garcia spent his life working as a high school principal in Brooklyn, a job that gave him a sense of purpose and kept him engaged with the world. A widower for six years now, he found comfort in his community: a bustling neighborhood of coffee shops, friendly clerks, and familiar faces at the corner market. After he retired, his days had a new rhythm: weekly card games, weekend trips to the library, and Sunday dinners with his daughter's family. Those dinners were his favorite, especially the ones where he told stories about his late wife, Sophia. Talking about her made her feel close again, like she was still laughing right there beside him.

Before the pandemic, Mr. Garcia had even started thinking about dating again. To him, finding someone new didn't mean letting go of Sophia. It meant honoring her memory while opening a new chapter. But then, in early 2020, the world shut down, and so did Mr. Garcia's tentative steps forward. His card games were canceled. The library doors closed. Even the cherished family dinners stopped, with his daughter worried about his health.

He understood her caution, he was in his seventies, after all. But the sudden silence hit hard. His house, once filled with voices and stories, felt like it had been muted.

As the weeks blurred into months, loneliness crept in like a slow fog. Phone calls and video chats helped, but they didn't fill the same emotional space as sitting across from someone in real life. Most days, he sat on his sofa with Oscar, his golden retriever, by his side. Oscar was nine now, with silver at the muzzle and a slower gait on their walks. Losing Oscar someday gnawed at Mr. Garcia. Oscar was their dog, adopted with Sophia, a living thread between past and present. More than a pet, Oscar was his last daily companion, the last witness to his shared life.

Over time, Mr. Garcia started to dim. His jokes faded. His voice lost its brightness, even on the phone. When his daughter finally arranged a socially distanced backyard visit, she noticed it right away. He looked thinner. Quieter. "Dad, are you okay?" she asked. And that was the moment he finally said it aloud. How hard the isolation had been. How, in many ways, it felt like losing Sophia all over again.

It was the first time he let himself admit it: he missed the little things. The soft background noise of life. The faces he waved to on the sidewalk. The warmth of someone simply sitting across from him. Without those things, the silence echoed louder than ever.

But that moment was also a turning point. His daughter began stopping by again, just for quick, masked visits. She encouraged him to call old friends. She printed a photo of Sophia and Oscar and placed it near his reading chair. Slowly, the fog began to lift.

Mr. Garcia started to feel like himself again. Not fully, but enough. Enough to remember that connection isn't a luxury. It's a lifeline. His story is a powerful reminder: loneliness can make even the most connected lives feel empty. But awareness and support, even in small doses, can bring us back.

Why Understanding Loneliness Matters

Understanding loneliness is one of the most important stops on the journey toward connection. Because when we treat it like a personal flaw or something we're supposed to just "get over," we miss what it's really trying to tell us.

Loneliness isn't a character defect. It's a signal.

A signal that something deeply human is out of sync. That you're wired for connection, and your body knows it's missing.

The science backs this up. Studies show that loneliness affects more than just your mood. It can impact everything from your immune system to your heart. And the longer it lingers, the heavier it gets.

Why Loneliness Hits So Hard

Think about it this way: our brains are wired to treat isolation like a real threat. Thousands of years ago, being alone wasn't just uncomfortable. It was dangerous. We needed our group to survive. Being alone meant vulnerability, predators, and exposure to danger. So our nervous system evolved to treat loneliness like an emergency.

Fast forward to today. No tigers, no hunting parties. But your nervous system doesn't know that. It still treats social disconnection as a crisis.

Your heart rate rises. Stress hormones surge. You feel on edge, like something's wrong, but you can't quite name what. It's your body saying, *Hey, you're supposed to have people around you.*

This is why chronic loneliness wears us down. When you're in a constant state of fight-or-flight, your system never fully relaxes. It quietly drains your energy, clouds your thinking, and slowly chips away at your health.

Loneliness is like a warning light on your emotional dashboard. It doesn't mean you're broken. It means you need care. And the earlier you notice it, the easier it is to respond.

Connection Isn't Just Comfort. It's Survival

On the flip side, strong relationships don't just feel good. They heal us.

Meaningful connection boosts emotional resilience. It helps us feel safe, grounded, and seen. It reduces stress, helps us sleep better, and allows us to recover from setbacks faster. When we feel truly connected to others, our bodies shift into a calmer state and work better because we're not in crisis mode.

This book isn't about perfect friend groups or fake social circles. It's here to help you rebuild something real. The kind of deep, honest connection that fuels you emotionally, mentally, and physically.

Physical Health Risks

- **Cardiovascular Disease:** Chronic loneliness increases your risk of heart disease and stroke. According to a major study published in the journal PLOS Medicine, loneliness can be as harmful to your heart as smoking 15 cigarettes a day.
- **Weakened Immune System:** Research shows that loneliness can affect your immune system at the genetic level, making it harder to stay physically healthy.
- **Increased Mortality Risk:** Loneliness can increase your risk of an early death. Studies have found that loneliness is as deadly as obesity or smoking.

Mental and Emotional Health Risks

Loneliness also deeply impacts emotional health, often leading to a vicious cycle: the lonelier you feel, the harder it is to reach out, which deepens isolation.

- **Depression and Anxiety:** Chronic loneliness is a major risk factor for both depression and anxiety, particularly for teens and young adults.

- **Cognitive Decline:** For older adults, loneliness has been linked to cognitive decline and an increased risk of conditions like Alzheimer's disease.
- **Suicide Rates:** Loneliness can also lead to suicidal thoughts and behaviors, especially in vulnerable groups like teens, veterans, and seniors.

You can't always choose your circumstances. However, you can start paying attention to the signals. And from there, one small step at a time, you can build your way back to connection.

When Loneliness Feeds on Itself

Loneliness doesn't always show up with flashing lights. It's not always loud or obvious. Sometimes, it sneaks in so quietly you don't even notice it at first. One missed invite. One unanswered text. One moment where you second-guess if you belong. It's subtle. But those little moments start to stack up. And before you realize what's happening, you're stuck in a loop. You feel disconnected, unsure of yourself, and wondering how things got so heavy.

The U.S. Surgeon General, Dr. Vivek Murthy, calls it a "reinforcing spiral." It starts with a single step back. Maybe you skip a gathering or convince yourself no one will notice if you don't show up. That one decision turns into two, then ten. You start thinking maybe you're just better off staying home, keeping to yourself. And with each quiet retreat, it gets harder to reach out. Eventually, isolation doesn't just feel familiar—it starts to feel like the only safe option.

The Stages of Loneliness

Stage 1: Initial Feelings of Isolation

It often starts innocently enough, maybe with a life change: a move, a breakup, or a shifting friend group. You skip an invitation, not because you don't care, but because you're tired or unsure if you'll fit in. You tell yourself:

It's just this one time.

I don't know anyone here.

Maybe it's better to stay in tonight.

That one skipped event feels harmless. You withdraw as a way to cope. But as time passes, it repeats. Not showing up becomes easier than facing the fear of being out of place.

Stage 2: Self-Doubt Creeps In

Loneliness turns into self-doubt and negative self-talk. The brain, trying to protect you, builds a wall. But it builds it from fear. That's when the inner voice kicks in:

Maybe people don't really want me around.

Maybe I'm not that interesting.

What started as a choice (*I'll stay in tonight*) becomes a belief:

I don't belong there anyway.

Stage 3: Shrinking the World

To avoid the awkwardness, you shrink your social world. You stop texting first. You mute group chats. Your phone buzzes, and you let it go. The longer the silence stretches, the louder your inner critic gets. One skipped event becomes two. Then five. Before long, not showing up becomes your default. Your absence goes unnoticed—or so you assume—and that assumption quietly feeds a thought:

Maybe I don't really matter to them.

Stage 4: Sadness and Anxiety

That's when the isolation worsens the feelings of loneliness, increasing sadness, shame, and anxiety around social interaction. Negative thoughts create fear of rejection, so you isolate more and avoid social interactions.

No one really understands me.

Reaching out now would only feel forced.

Stage 5: Perception Becomes Biased

Our brains are brilliant storytellers, but they're not always fair. When we feel disconnected, we start to interpret neutral moments as rejection. This increases withdrawal and mistrust toward others, reinforcing the cycle of isolation.

Your friend takes a little too long to reply?

They must be done with me.

You see your coworkers hanging out without you?

I'm being excluded.

These aren't facts, they're fear-fueled interpretations. But in the moment, they feel real. Loneliness rewires the way we perceive the world. It puts us in protection mode.

Stage 6: Self-Fulfilling Prophecy

Feeling unworthy of social connection becomes a reality as self-isolation takes hold.

I'm just not good at making friends.

Maybe I'm meant to be alone.

This is the final loop: accepting isolation as inevitable, feeling "stuck" in loneliness.

But here's the truth: you weren't always this way. And you don't have to stay in this place. Loneliness might be persuasive, but it isn't permanent.

Here's what I want you to remember: loneliness isn't a character flaw. It's not a failure. And it's definitely not permanent.

You don't have to fix who you are. You need to listen to what loneliness is really saying: *I need connection.*

And that's something you can do, one small shift at a time. You don't have to become someone else to feel connected. You just have to stop believing the story that says you're not enough.

Erin's Story

It wasn't that she didn't want her friends to be happy. She did. In fact, Erin was going to be a bridesmaid at her best friend's wedding next summer, and she was even helping plan a baby shower for another friend. She put on a smile, bought the gifts, and gave heartfelt congratulations, but deep down, she felt like a fraud. Inside, there was a knot of jealousy and envy she couldn't untangle. She hated feeling this way, and it only made the emptiness worse. How could she be so happy for her friends while simultaneously feeling so horrible about herself?

Erin had always been a little on the shy side, not naturally outgoing, but not completely withdrawn either. She liked her close-knit group of friends and usually felt comfortable in familiar settings. But after the breakup and watching everyone around her move forward with relationships, her natural shyness had morphed into something else. She started to feel anxious in social situations, especially around people she didn't know well or in environments where she felt like she was the odd one out. Her anxiety had started creeping up in unexpected ways. Even when her friends invited her to parties or social events, she found herself coming up with excuses to stay home.

It wasn't that she didn't want to go, but the thought of being surrounded by couples or new people made her feel small and insignificant. She couldn't stand the idea of having to answer questions like "Are you seeing anyone?" or, worse, sitting alone while everyone else paired up. More and more, she found herself declining invitations and staying in. It was easier to just avoid it all than to face those uncomfortable feelings of isolation in a crowd.

Erin's friends kept trying to cheer her up, telling her she was beautiful and that it was just a matter of time before she found her "special someone." But honestly, Erin wasn't buying it anymore. Their words felt kind of hollow, like clichés they were just saying to make her feel better. It was tough for her to accept that they really understood her situation. They had their own lives filled with love and partners, while she had to face an empty apartment every evening. Scrolling through social media didn't help either; seeing everyone else moving forward just made her feel even more stuck.

Social media had become her worst enemy. Every time she opened Instagram or Facebook, it felt like she was bombarded with images of people living the life she dreamed of—engagement rings, wedding dresses, honeymoon photos, baby bumps. Everyone had someone except her. She couldn't help but wonder if this was it for her, if she'd always be the one standing on the sidelines, watching everyone else find happiness.

The isolation was starting to convince her that she was the problem. Maybe she just wasn't cut out for relationships. Maybe she wasn't good enough. Her confidence, once vibrant, had dulled to a flicker. She didn't even feel like trying to meet anyone anymore. Dating apps felt like a dangerous landscape of rejection, and the idea of trying to put herself out there once more was draining. Erin started to believe that love just wasn't in the cards for her. Maybe she'd never find the right guy, never get married, never have the family she'd always dreamed of.

And that's what loneliness does. It doesn't just make you feel isolated—it makes you doubt yourself. It makes you believe that maybe the reason you're alone is because there's something wrong with you. For Erin, the loneliness was more than just an empty feeling. It was a deep, growing insecurity, a belief that she would never be enough for anyone.

What matters most isn't how long we've felt it, but how we choose to respond. Understanding it is the first step toward changing it.

What This Means: Loneliness isn't just a passing feeling; it's a mirror. It reflects how we think, feel, and connect. It can distort how we see ourselves and others, pulling us deeper into isolation, the longer it goes unaddressed. Recognizing it as more than just "feeling off" is how we begin to shift it.

Why It Matters: Left unchecked, loneliness reshapes our confidence, our social energy, and even our health. But awareness gives you back your power. When you understand what loneliness does to your mind and body, you can stop blaming yourself and start building something better.

What Comes Next: You're not stuck. With the right tools, you can interrupt the cycle and start reconnecting, first with yourself and then with others. In the next chapter, you'll learn how balanced emotional energy is the foundation for real connection and lasting confidence.

Chapter 2

The Power of Balanced Energy to Change Your Life

"We are not meant to go through life alone.
True connection starts by
restoring balance within ourselves."

I still remember when I began my career as a clinician. I was an intern at a mental health clinic during grad school, excited, motivated, and ready to learn. I had a strong rapport with my supervisor, and thanks to her guidance, I felt confident in my client sessions.

But around my colleagues? That was a different story.

They were friendly, always smiling, and often invited me to join them for lunch. On the surface, it seemed like I was being included. But inside, I couldn't shake the feeling that I didn't belong. I told myself I was just "the new intern," too inexperienced to really be part of the group.

Have you ever felt like that?

I used to hide in my office during lunch, convincing myself I had too much work or just wouldn't know what to say. Honestly, it wasn't my colleagues leaving me out. It was me doing it to myself. That little bit of self-doubt turned into a cycle. I acted like I didn't belong, so of course, I felt like I didn't.

It wasn't until much later that I understood just how much my energy was shaping those interactions. My fear and self-doubt weren't just internal. They showed up in my body language, tone, and presence. The story I told myself—that I didn't belong—was actually keeping me from belonging. No one else was doing that to me. I was doing it to myself.

That experience became one of my earliest lessons in emotional energy: The way we manage our inner state shapes the quality of our relationships. It can be the difference between loneliness and connection.

What Is Energy?

Energy isn't just about whether you feel tired or alert. It's the fuel behind how you show up in the world. It affects your mood, your presence, and your ability to connect with people. It shapes how you experience your day and how others experience you.

DEFINITION

Energy is the invisible force that shapes how we think, feel, and relate to others. It colors our mood, influences our actions, and affects how people respond to us.

It moves in two key directions:

- **Internal Energy**

  This is your emotional capacity—your thoughts, emotions, and physical state that create your internal atmosphere. Are you calm? Drained? Anxious? Energized? Your internal state colors how you see yourself and how you show up for others.

- **External Energy**

  This is your vibe—your posture, tone, and presence. It's the subtle energy others pick up on, often before you say a word.

Understanding your energy is like reading your own weather forecast. The more tuned in you are to your inner atmosphere, the easier it is to adjust it. And when you know what you're working with, you can show up more intentionally in every conversation, every interaction.

When both parts of your energy are aligned—when you feel grounded on the inside and open on the outside—people feel it. You radiate calm, connection, and confidence without even trying.

Balanced Energy

When your **emotional capacity** and your **external vibe** are both in balance, you create the conditions for trust and ease. You're less likely to be reactive and more likely to be present. Your energy becomes the bridge between you and others.

Let's break it down a bit more.

Emotional Capacity

Like an internal battery, this is your internal reserve of resilience and energy. High emotional capacity means you're better equipped to handle stress, adapt to social situations, and engage without burning out. It's influenced by:

- **Nervous system regulation:** Balance between stress and relaxation responses (sympathetic and parasympathetic).
- **Emotional intelligence:** Awareness of your feelings and the ability to self-regulate.
- **Physical well-being:** Sleep, nutrition, and movement
- **Supportive relationships:** Social connection that restores and sustains you.
- **Life experience:** Learning from challenges and building inner strength.

Think of your emotional capacity like a container. It holds everything you're feeling and processing in a given moment. When that container fills up with stress, grief, or just too much stimulation, it gets harder to stay grounded. You might snap at your partner, shut down at work, or zone out during conversations. It doesn't mean you're bad at relationships. It just means your nervous system is running low.

But when your emotional capacity is high, everything feels lighter. You're more patient, more curious, and you actually hear people instead of just waiting to speak. Silence doesn't rattle you, and you're better able to stay present and connected with the people around you.

The Vibe

This is the energy you give off: your tone, your posture, your presence. It's the atmosphere you bring into every interaction. You might not notice it, but others feel it right away.

When your emotional tank is low on the inside, it's harder to project warmth, patience, or genuine interest on the outside. We've all had those days when we're stressed, drained, or anxious, and the people around us seem to pick up on it. That's not your imagination. Your nervous system is constantly signaling your state, even before you speak.

But when your internal and external energy are aligned, you show up with a sense of calm, confidence, and authenticity. Connection feels easier, not because you're trying harder, but because you're in tune with yourself.

Balanced energy is the harmony between your inner state and the way you interact with the world.

Balanced energy doesn't mean you're always calm or cheerful. It means you're steady enough to handle discomfort without letting it spill onto everyone else. You've got just enough space between what happens and how you respond to choose how you want to show up. That's where real power lives.

Your internal emotional capacity and your external vibe are deeply connected. Together, they shape how you experience yourself and how others experience you. When your inner reserves are strong and your outer presence is open, people feel it. You don't need to force confidence. You just feel more at ease, more grounded, and more available. That's balanced energy in motion. It's subtle, but incredibly magnetic.

This isn't about being in a good mood all the time or saying the perfect thing. It's about being real, even when life feels messy. You're not performing. You're not trying to impress. You're just grounded enough to show up as yourself, and that kind of presence makes connection easier for everyone.

Balanced energy helps you tune in, listen, and respond with openness. Think about the last time a conversation just clicked. It probably felt easy, maybe even fun, like time disappeared. That's not luck. That's your nervous system syncing with someone else's, creating a sense of emotional safety.

Connection is where science meets soul.
It's not magic.
It's your body saying, I feel safe here.

But when your energy is off, tense, shut down, or running on empty, people pick up on it. You might not mean to, but it can come across as guarded or distant. That's not a flaw. It's a signal that your system needs care.

The moment you start interacting with someone else, your energy shifts from internal to shared. That shift—the way you read, respond, and reflect back—is what brings connection to life. It's not random. It follows a rhythm. A give-and-take. A loop.

And when your energy is balanced, that loop flows. You feel better. Others feel safer. And connection happens naturally.

The Cycle of Connection

Here's something most people don't realize: Your emotional energy is contagious. The way you feel on the inside shapes how people feel around you.

We all carry an internal state: your thoughts, feelings, stress levels, sense of safety. And that internal state influences how open, warm, and connected you seem on the outside.

That's what creates the Cycle of Connection. There are two emotional feedback loops at play:

- **The Upward Cycle of Connection** builds confidence, synchrony, and belonging. When you feel safe and grounded, you're more open, your body language invites others in, and people are more likely to respond with warmth. That connection makes you feel seen and strengthens your confidence to keep showing up.

- **The Downward Cycle of Loneliness** does the opposite. When you feel overwhelmed, anxious, or insecure, it changes the energy you bring into a room. Maybe you don't make eye contact. Maybe your shoulders are tense, or your smile doesn't reach your eyes. And when others sense that guardedness, they might pull back too, feeding the very loneliness you were trying to escape.

Each cycle reinforces itself.

THE CYCLE OF CONNECTION

The Cycle of Connection is about how our internal state influences our ability to connect with others. It consists of two opposing cycles:

↑ **The Upward Cycle of Connection**
Synchrony & Belonging

↓ **The Downward Cycle of Loneliness**
Disconnection & Isolation

Each loop fuels itself. One draws you into deeper belonging. The other into quiet withdrawal.

This isn't about personality. It's about your emotional state. Whether you're extroverted or introverted, you can still find yourself stuck in either loop—depending on how you feel inside. The good news is, you can break the cycle. You can shift it. But first, you have to notice which one you're in.

The Upward Cycle of Connection

Confidence → Safety → Belonging

When your internal world feels steady, the outside world responds in kind. You feel grounded, like you're enough just as you are. And that sense of calm confidence comes across in everything: how you carry yourself, how you listen, how you engage.

It's not about being loud or outgoing. It's about feeling safe enough in your own skin to be present with others.

That presence builds trust. It says, "I'm here. I see you." And when people feel seen, they open up. That shared openness, when two nervous systems settle into the same rhythm, that's synchrony.

Synchrony is what happens when:
- A conversation flows without effort
- You feel "in sync" with someone else's energy
- You both laugh at the same moment without planning to

This is where belonging begins. Not with grand gestures, but in these subtle moments of connecting..

And every time you experience one of those moments, it leaves a trace. It builds your social confidence. It makes the next interaction feel easier. You carry that energy with you into the next space, and suddenly, the upward spiral has begun.

Real-Life Moment: Erica on the Train

Every morning, Erica took the same commuter train into the city. She usually kept to herself, earbuds in, head down, scrolling her phone. The train was full of strangers, all packed together but emotionally distant.

One particularly crowded morning, she gave up her seat to an older woman standing nearby. It wasn't a big gesture, just instinct. The woman smiled and said, "You remind me of my granddaughter." They exchanged a few more words before the next stop. Nothing deep. Just… human.

But that brief interaction nudged something in Erica.

The next morning, she looked up instead of down. She made eye contact with the regulars she saw every day. A man across the aisle nodded at her. Another offered a polite "good morning."

No deep conversations. No instant friendships. But the vibe changed. So did her energy. The train ride didn't feel as heavy, as isolating. That one moment of kindness had started a ripple. A quiet loop of presence, visibility, and mutual regard. That's a connection too.

She stopped feeling like just another stranger on the train. She felt part of something again. That tiny moment reminded her that connection doesn't always come in big, dramatic waves. Sometimes it starts with a glance. A smile. A simple choice to look up and let the world in.

The Downward Cycle of Loneliness

Anxiety → Withdrawal → Isolation

Just like connection builds on itself, so does loneliness. When your internal energy feels anxious, depleted, or uncertain, it shows up on the outside, even when you try to hide it.

Maybe you avoid eye contact. Maybe your voice tightens. Maybe you start second-guessing every word. You might not notice it's happening, but others can. The nervous system is incredibly sensitive to subtle shifts in tone, posture, and presence.

When people around you pick up on that tension, they might unconsciously pull back. Not because they don't like you, but because the interaction doesn't feel easy or safe. And when that happens, it can feel like confirmation of your worst fears:

See? I don't belong here.

Nobody really wants me around.

That discouragement feeds the next layer: withdrawal. You might cancel plans. Stop reaching out. Fade quietly into the background. And the longer the silence stretches, the heavier the loneliness feels. What started as a flicker becomes a pattern.

The most painful part? You might start confusing the feeling with who you are.

It's not just *I feel disconnected*. It becomes *I am disconnected*.

> Loneliness rewires the way we perceive the world.
> It makes neutral faces seem cold.
> It makes missed texts feel like rejection.
> It makes "alone" feel like "unworthy."

You can see this pattern unfold in everyday moments.

Real-Life Moment: Tyler at the Family Gathering

Tyler had always been a little shy, especially around his extended family. Big holiday gatherings made him anxious. Too much noise, too much small talk, too much pressure to fit in. This year felt even harder. Everyone seemed caught up in their own conversations, swapping stories, laughing about memories Tyler wasn't part of.

At first, he tried to join in. He hovered near his cousins, nodding along to jokes he didn't really get. But after a few minutes of feeling invisible, he gave up. He found a corner, glued himself to his phone, and waited for the afternoon to pass.

Nobody came over, not because they didn't care, but because Tyler's closed-off body language and quietness made it hard to approach. From the outside, it probably looked like he wanted to be left alone.

Inside, Tyler felt forgotten.

They don't even notice I'm here, he thought.

I don't really belong with them.

By the end of the day, he wasn't just feeling lonely. He was starting to believe that loneliness was all he could expect.

But even as he sat there, he began to wonder, what if next time, he tried something different?

Interrupting the Downward Cycle

The downward cycle of loneliness can feel heavy. It can convince you that disconnection is permanent and that belonging is something reserved for other people. But here's the truth:

Cycles are patterns, not destinies.

And patterns can be changed.

Even the smallest action can begin to interrupt the spiral.

You don't have to fix everything at once. You don't have to fake confidence or force yourself into overwhelming situations. You just have to create one small shift, a crack where hope can slip in.

It might look like:

- Making eye contact with someone when you would normally look away.
- Replying to a text you've been avoiding, even with just a few words.
- Smiling at the cashier, even if it feels awkward.
- Showing up to the gathering, even if you stay only for twenty minutes.

Each small act chips away at the isolation.

Each act reminds your nervous system: It's safe to connect.

Each act strengthens the upward cycle.

You don't need to feel completely ready. You just need to take one small step toward connection, and trust that it matters because it does.

We all need to feel that we belong,
that we're seen, valued, and accepted.
Managing your emotional energy
helps create that sense of belonging.
**When your presence radiates openness and calm,
it draws people toward you.**

Energy isn't just how you feel. It's what others feel from you. When you understand the difference between balanced and unbalanced energy, you stop wondering why some interactions feel easy and others fall flat. Connection doesn't start with effort. It starts with awareness.

What This Means: Balanced energy is the foundation of connection. When your inner world feels steady, your outer presence becomes more grounded, open, and inviting. People don't just respond to your words; they respond to your vibe.

Why It Matters: Confidence isn't about performance; it's about presence. Unbalanced energy, like stress, self-doubt, or distraction, can cloud how others experience you and how you experience yourself. But when you tune into your internal state, you create space for something different.

What Comes Next: Before your next social interaction, take a moment and ask: What energy am I bringing in? A 10-second check-in can help you show up with calm, curiosity, or clarity. Small shifts like this ripple outward.

Chapter 3

Interpersonal Synchrony

"When two people truly connect, it's as if their hearts and minds beat together in perfect harmony."

One evening, I was walking my dog and I noticed the two teen girls at the end of the block walking towards us. They weren't talking much (unusual for teen girls), but something about the way they moved together caught my attention. Their steps matched, their postures mirrored each other, and every now and then, they shared a glance or a quiet laugh. It wasn't loud or showy—it was subtle, but undeniable. They were in sync.

That moment reminded me of something we often forget: we're always moving in silent rhythm with those around us. Whether we're joking with a friend, leaning into a hug, or sharing eye contact with a stranger in line, we're syncing. Not just socially, but emotionally, and even physiologically. This isn't some romantic notion. It's biology, behavior, and belonging working together in real time.

But the opposite is true too. When we're out of sync—when a conversation feels forced, or loneliness creeps in—it can leave us feeling drained, disconnected, and even isolated. Understanding why this happens and how to shift back into alignment is the key to building better relationships.

This chapter explores the power of interpersonal synchrony, how it impacts our emotional and physiological well-being, and practical ways to cultivate synchrony in everyday life.

What Is Interpersonal Synchrony?

Interpersonal synchrony is the beautiful way two people can naturally fall into rhythm during their interactions. It's that moment when you share a laugh at just the right time, mirror each other's body language, feel emotionally "on the same page," or instinctively match each other's pace on a walk. These tiny moments may seem small, but they make conversations and connections feel richer and more meaningful.

This subtle, often unnoticed harmony is the bridge that transforms balanced energy into connection.

Science has a lot to say about this invisible dance. There's so much happening behind the scenes that we might not even

---

DEFINITION

Interpersonal Synchrony

Interpersonal synchrony is the dynamic flow of emotional energy between people that creates connection.

notice. When we sync up with other people, it's like our brains, bodies, and emotions start to align.

Social psychologists have found that when we sync up like this, we're more likely to feel connected, trust the other person, and even become more generous. Neuroscience backs this up too, showing that synchrony isn't just about what's said, but about a deeper exchange of emotional and nonverbal signals. It's in the tone of our voice, our facial expressions, our posture, and even in the rhythms of our heartbeat.

The most amazing part? This kind of syncing often happens without us realizing it. Yet when it does, it creates a powerful sense of closeness, comfort, and belonging.

And it's not just limited to body language. Interpersonal synchrony shows up in romantic chemistry, best friend moments, group dynamics in sports, and even therapy sessions. It's one of those quiet but powerful forces that helps us shift from feeling awkward to feeling truly connected.

How is it that we can step into a room and immediately sense the mood? The tension is so thick you want to run back out. Or excitement that pulls you in and makes you smile before you even know why. Or if someone else walks in, and the vibe suddenly changes? How powerful is the person (or your dog) who comes in a great mood and is clearly happy to see you? Or vice versa.

Emotions don't just stay inside us; they spill outward. They pass through tone, posture, expression, and presence. A single look can lift or deflate a room. Think of a teacher's stern glance or someone's unexpected belly laugh during a quiet meeting.

These small signals shape the atmosphere before a word is even spoken.

Like the legendary "mom look" that can stop kids (and adults) in their tracks, no words needed. This powerful stare can silence a room. It conveys a range of messages, from "I'm watching you" to "You're in trouble," and even "I love you."

Or have you ever been in a class or work meeting that had everyone feeling pretty drained? But then, someone cracks a joke, and suddenly the whole room bursts into laughter. Just like that, the vibe totally changes. That's what they mean by emotional contagion!

Emotional contagion works both ways.
Negativity can spread just as easily.
Ever had a great day ruined by someone else's bad mood?
That's why managing your emotional energy—
what you bring into a room—is so critical.

Synchrony doesn't stop at the brain. It moves through the body as well. Studies have shown that when people are deeply connected, their physiological responses, such as heart rate and breathing patterns, begin to align. This phenomenon, known as human physiological synchrony, has been observed in couples, close friends, and even strangers engaging in meaningful interactions.

The next time you have a heartfelt conversation with someone, see if you notice that you are breathing in rhythm.

This isn't a coincidence. It's your body syncing to create a sense of harmony and connection.

> **THE SCIENCE BEHIND IT**
>
> ### Social Anxiety and the Challenges of Synchrony
>
> For people with social anxiety, synchrony can feel out of reach. It's not that they don't want to connect. It's that their focus turns inward. Instead of feeling the natural back-and-forth of connection, they're tuned into their own doubts, worried how they're coming across. This inner static blocks the emotional signal, making meaningful interaction feel harder than it should.
>
> ### Heart Rate Synchrony
>
> Social anxiety has been linked to disruptions in heart rate synchrony (HR synchrony) and the alignment of physiological responses between individuals. People with high social anxiety often struggle to reach the same level of HR synchrony as those without anxiety. This can increase feelings of isolation and disconnection.
>
> **Practical Insight:** Understanding this challenge is the first step toward overcoming it. Small, intentional actions like maintaining eye contact or mirroring someone's body language can help restore synchrony, even in anxious situations.

Common Pitfalls

If connecting with others feels so natural, why can it sometimes be tough? It's not just about being on the same page. It's also about tackling the things that can throw us off. Here are some of the common pitfalls that can get in the way of syncing up with other people.

Why Social Anxiety Disrupts Synchrony

When you're socially anxious, your brain goes into overdrive. Instead of being present and picking up on what's happening around you, you start overthinking everything: how you look, what to say, whether you're making it weird. That mental noise makes it hard to connect with people in real time. That disconnection doesn't just feel bad, it actually shows up in your body. Researchers call it heart rate synchrony, which is a fancy way of saying our physiological rhythms align when we're truly connected with someone. But when you're anxious? That alignment shuts down.

Let me show you what this looks like in real life.

The studio was warm and bright, and the music had that classy, jazzy vibe that was supposed to feel fun, but to Ava, it felt like pressure. Couples were already stepping onto the dance floor, laughing and adjusting their stances. It was supposed to be a lighthearted date night. But Ava couldn't relax.

She stood next to her boyfriend, Daniel, arms stiff at her sides. Her smile felt fake, like something she had to put on so nobody would know how uncomfortable she was.

Daniel looked over and gave her hand a quick squeeze. "We've got this," he said.

She nodded. "Totally," she replied, even though everything inside her said the opposite.

The instructor started walking everyone through a simple box step. The other couples were clumsy, sure, but they were moving. They were having fun. Ava, on the other hand, was stuck in her head. *What if I trip? What if I do it wrong? What if everyone sees how awkward I am?*

As the lesson picked up, Daniel gently tried to lead her into the rhythm. But Ava kept hesitating. Every time she started to follow his lead, a voice in her brain would chime in: *You're off. You're too slow. He probably regrets bringing you.*

She couldn't stay in sync, not because she didn't want to, but because her brain was hijacking the moment. Her thoughts were louder than the music.

Daniel glanced at her. "You okay?" he asked, keeping his voice low.

"Yeah," she said, forcing a quick smile. "I just… need a second."

The thing was, her body was right there on the dance floor, but emotionally? She was miles away. While the other couples moved with each other—laughing, adjusting, connecting—Ava felt like she was trying to perform. Like she had to earn the right to belong in the room.

Daniel tried to help her get back into rhythm. He was patient. But the mood had already shifted. They weren't really dancing together anymore. They were trying to navigate around Ava's anxiety, and that tension made it impossible to get into sync.

Ava wasn't disconnected because she didn't care; she was disconnected because her anxiety was running the show.

And that's what social anxiety does. It shuts off the part of your brain that can connect in real-time and replaces it with self-doubt and overthinking. Even in a room full of music, smiles, and opportunity, you can still feel like you're completely alone.

Emotional Mismatch: When Energy Levels Clash

Sometimes, you're just not in the same emotional gear. Maybe you're riding the high of good news, and the other person is emotionally drained. It's like dancing to two different songs. No one's wrong, it just doesn't flow.

Example: Imagine coming home after an amazing day at work, eager to share your excitement, only to find your partner stressed out from their own tough day. The mismatch in emotional energy makes it hard to find common ground, even though you both care deeply about each other.

How to Address It: Start by acknowledging the other person's emotional state. Phrases like "It sounds like you've had a rough day, want to talk about it?" can create space for alignment without dismissing your own emotions.

Miscommunication: When Words Get in the Way

Things fall apart fast when someone takes what you said the wrong way. Maybe it's your tone, your choice of words, or just a bad read on a message. Even small misunderstandings can make the whole interaction feel weird.

Example: You send a text that you think is funny, "Wow, running late again?" But they read it as a jab. Now they feel judged, you're confused, and the whole vibe gets derailed before the conversation even starts.

How to Address It: If things feel off, hit pause. Ask something like, "Hey, that came out wrong. Can I rephrase?" or "That was a joke. Did it land weird?" A quick check-in can fix the misread before it turns into a mess.

Digital Disconnection: The Tech Barrier

Texts and video calls give us the words, but strip out all the stuff that makes the connection feel real. A frozen screen or awkward delay kills the flow. Even when everything works technically, it can still feel cold and disconnected.

Example: You hop on a Zoom with a co-worker, and it's just... off. Delays, frozen faces, no body language. It's like talking to a wall, even if the words are right.

How to Address It: When you can, meet in person. If you're stuck on a screen, lean into verbal cues like "That makes sense" or "I totally get that" so the other person knows you're tuned in.

Power Dynamics: Unequal Roles in Relationships

When one person has all the control, at home, work, or anywhere else, it throws the balance off. It's hard to feel connected when your voice isn't getting heard.

Example: At home, one parent does all the talking and decision-making. The teen never gets a real chance to chime in. Eventually, they shut down, because what's the point in speaking if no one's really listening?

How to Address It: Want to even things out? Ask for their input, really listen, and let your body language, like eye contact and nods, show them you care. That small shift builds trust fast.

Overthinking: The Enemy of Presence

Ever been in a conversation but completely stuck in your head? You're overthinking every word, wondering how you sound, and second-guessing yourself in real time. That mental loop blocks connection completely.

Example: You're out on a date, but instead of just enjoying it, you're too busy stressing over whether they're having fun, if you're saying the right things, or if you should smile more. You're not connecting, you're performing.

How to Address It: Focus on them, not you. Ask questions. Really listen. Remind yourself: connection isn't about saying the perfect thing, it's about being real in the moment.

Distracted Presence: The Multitasking Barrier

If you're checking your phone while someone's talking, they notice. Even if you don't mean it, when your attention is somewhere else, it kills the connection fast.

Example: You're out to lunch with a friend, but you keep sneaking looks at your email. They feel it, even if they don't say anything. The conversation loses momentum.

How to Address It: Put the phone down. Clear your mind. Look them in the eye and actually listen. That's how you show someone they matter.

Emotional Walls: Fear of Vulnerability

When you've been burned before, it's easy to keep your guard up. You don't share much, and that makes connection hard. People can't sync with a wall.

Example: You're at a party, but you're stuck in small talk mode. You don't open up because you're scared of saying the wrong thing or being judged. So even though you're surrounded by people, you feel completely disconnected.

How to Address It: Start small. Share something light but real. Watch how people respond. That's how trust builds, and that's how you get back into sync.

Cultural Differences: Navigating Unfamiliar Norms

What's normal for you might be totally off for someone else. Different cultures have different ways of connecting, and if you're not aware of that, things can get awkward fast.

Example: You're on a business trip and jump into a meeting with your usual get-to-the-point style. But the local team moves more slowly, more formally. Now it feels like you're pushing too hard, too fast.

How to Address It: Pay attention. Read the room. Show respect for how others connect. A little flexibility goes a long way toward building real rapport.

Mismatched Expectations: When Goals Don't Align

Sometimes, you're both coming in with totally different goals. You're ready for a deep talk and they just want to keep it casual. You walk away feeling unheard. They walk away confused.

Example: You head to a family dinner thinking it's a chance to talk about something that's been on your mind. But everyone's joking around, passing food, and sticking to safe topics. You leave feeling like you didn't get what you came for.

How to Address It: Be upfront. Say, "Hey, I've got something I'd love to talk about tonight if there's a good time." That heads-up gives you both a chance to get on the same page.

HOW YOU CAN DO IT

- ✔ **Start Small:** Synchrony doesn't have to mean deep conversations or big gestures. Smile at someone. Share a quick laugh with a coworker. Little moments of connection matter.
- ✔ **Mirror Body Language:** Subtle mimicry, like mirroring someone's posture or tone, builds rapport and alignment. Just don't overdo it.
- ✔ **Engage in Shared Activities:** Whether it's cooking, walking, or dancing, shared activities naturally create synchrony by aligning your movements and focus.
- ✔ **Practice Empathy:** Listen deeply, validate what others are feeling, and reflect back their emotions. This creates emotional alignment and trust.
- ✔ **Create Social Rituals:** Consistent check-ins, like a weekly dinner or a quick text, keep your connections alive and strong.

Connection isn't about perfect timing or flawless words. It's about showing up fully and letting yourself be moved by the moment. Synchrony happens not when we try harder, but when we stop trying to control every beat and instead listen for the shared rhythm between us.

What This Means: Synchrony is the invisible thread that makes relationships feel natural. You don't need to be perfect. Just be present. Trust the moment to guide you. Real connection isn't forced—it's felt.
Why It Matters: When you're in sync with someone, even briefly, your emotional energy gets a boost. You feel seen, supported, and grounded. Understanding how synchrony works, and how it breaks, helps you stay connected more consistently, even in tough moments.
What Comes Next: Think back to a moment when you felt truly "in sync" with someone. What made it possible? Now, think about how you might invite that same energy into your next conversation through presence, attention, and a willingness to align.

Connection isn't about saying the right thing.
It's about showing up, tuning in,
and letting the moment lead.

Chapter 4

The Science of Connection and Happiness

"The two things that predict whether or not you're happy are how much time you spend with friends and family, and how much time you're physically around other people."
— Dr. Laurie Santos

Have you ever noticed how good you feel after a deep conversation or a shared laugh with a friend? That warm, contented glow you feel isn't just emotional. It's chemical. Our brains are wired to crave connection. It's not just about enjoying other people's company; it's about survival. For thousands of years, we've relied on each other for safety, resources, and support. This drive for connection is hardwired into our brains, making social interactions feel deeply rewarding.

When we engage with others, our **brain's reward system** releases feel-good chemicals that create a powerful sense of closeness and joy. **Dopamine** energizes and motivates us, while

oxytocin builds trust and emotional warmth. Together, they act like the brain's social fuel, giving us that rush of satisfaction after a good conversation or a sense of calm when we're around people we care about. These chemical surges don't just feel good. They actively wire our brains for connection, reinforcing future interactions through subtle emotional cues like shared smiles and attuned gestures. In other words, connection isn't just nice, it's biologically rewarding.

This reward system is why social motivation is so powerful. When you reach out to a friend, share a meal with family, or even make small talk with a stranger, your brain reinforces those actions with a chemical "reward." It's like your brain saying, "Yes, this is good, do more of this." Over time, these positive social experiences create a feedback loop: connection fuels happiness, and happiness fuels more connection.

The reward system is so important that it's tied directly to our well-being. Studies show that people with strong social bonds are healthier, happier, and even live longer. Connection isn't just nice to have—it's essential.

The Happiness Formula

Let's start with a truth that's both simple and profound: humans are wired for connection. We're not just social creatures; we're biologically programmed to thrive when we're with others. Research consistently shows that the two biggest predictors of happiness are how much time you spend with friends and family, and how much time you spend physically around other people.

> **THE SCIENCE BEHIND IT**
>
> **How We Align With Others**
>
> At its core, interpersonal synchrony is about alignment—not just emotional, but physiological and neurological too. When we interact with others, our bodies and brains begin to mirror each other in remarkable ways.
>
> **Mirror Neurons**
>
> One of the most fascinating discoveries in neuroscience is the role of mirror neurons. These are specialized brain cells that fire both when we perform an action and when we observe someone else performing the same action. For example, when you see someone smile, your mirror neurons activate, encouraging you to smile back. This neural mirroring helps us understand and empathize with others, making it a cornerstone of interpersonal synchrony.
>
> **Example:** Picture a mother and her baby. When the mother smiles, the baby's mirror neurons activate, prompting the baby to smile in return. This simple exchange isn't just adorable, it's a foundational building block of emotional connection.

That doesn't mean being the life of the party or constantly surrounded by people. Even small moments of connection, like a chat with a neighbor, a call with a loved one, or simply being in the same space as others, can have a big impact on your happiness. Why? Because when you're around people, your brain gets a boost.

Here's how it works: when you interact with someone, your brain lights up like fireworks on the Fourth of July—bright, energized, and fully alive. Brain cells called **mirror neurons** fire, helping you pick up on what the other person is feeling. But they don't just help you understand emotions, they actually let you feel them too. Have you ever noticed how you automatically wave hello (or yawn) when someone else does? That's your mirror neurons at work, pulling you into the moment and making you feel a sense of connection. Even dogs often yawn when someone they love yawns. This mirroring points to shared emotional responses, showing that connection —even across species—is deeply wired.

And it doesn't stop there. Those emotional sparks are your brain's way of rewarding the moment, helping you feel happier, calmer, and more connected. That's why a deep conversation or a shared laugh doesn't just feel good, it recharges you. That's exactly why real-time connection matters more than we often realize.

Elena's Story: Why Real-Time Matters

Elena recently moved to a new city for work, leaving behind her family and close friends. At first, she tried to stay connected through texts and social media, sending quick updates and liking posts. But no matter how many messages she sent, she felt... off like something was missing.

One weekend, a coworker invited Elena out for brunch with a few others. She hesitated. Meeting new people felt like too much effort. But something made her say yes. Two hours and countless laughs later, Elena walked home feeling a sense of warmth and ease she hadn't felt in months. It wasn't just the conversation; it was the presence, the laughter, the shared experience.

The next day, Elena reflected on why texting didn't feel the same. The answer was simple: **real-time connection had activated something in her that texts couldn't touch**. At that moment, she realized that the happiness she experienced was about the quality of her interactions.

Elena's story perfectly illustrates how the happiness formula and interpersonal synchrony work together. By choosing to accept the invitation, she created an opportunity to be around others and begin forming new friendships. Beneath the surface, the powerful influence of interpersonal synchrony helped her connect with those around her on emotional, physical, and neurological levels, which also gave her brain's reward system a nice boost. Here's what was happening:

- **Mirror Neurons at Work:** When she laughed with her new friends, her brain synced up with theirs, creating a sense of shared understanding and belonging.
- **Oxytocin Release:** Being physically present helped her feel safe and emotionally connected, building trust with the group.
- **Dopamine Boost:** The energy of the interaction left her feeling uplifted and motivated to connect again.

"While virtual tools have their place, nothing compares to the rich, fulfilling experience of being physically present with others."

	FACE-TO-FACE	VIRTUAL
Emotional Connection	Strong (eye contact, body language, touch)	Moderate (limited nonverbal cues)
Energy Exchange	Replenishing (direct vibe sharing)	Neutral or draining (screen fatigue)
Accessibility	Requires effort (travel, planning)	Highly convenient
Depth of Interaction	Deep (richer conversations)	Surface-level (shorter, transactional)

Why Texting Falls Short

Remember a time you texted a friend, maybe to vent, get support, or just feel a little closer? Maybe you waited for their response, hoping for a quick reply. When it finally came, did it feel satisfying, or did it leave you wanting more?

For many of us, texting has become the default mode of communication. It's convenient, quick, and feels like an easy way to stay connected. But here's the catch: while texting can increase the desire for connection, it rarely fulfills it. Instead of feeling closer to the person on the other side of the screen, we're often left feeling lonelier.

Texting creates the illusion of connection, but it lacks the key ingredients that make communication truly meaningful: tone, body language, and real-time feedback.

- **No Tone or Emotion:** Without vocal inflection or facial expressions, texts can feel flat, or worse, misinterpreted.
- **Delays:** Unlike a real-time conversation, texting introduces delays that can disrupt the flow of connection.

- **Emotional Gaps:** When you're texting, you're not getting the warmth of a laugh or the reassurance of a smile. It's like trying to stay warm with a single thread instead of a full blanket.

Texting is great for quick logistics—like figuring out what time to meet up—but it doesn't really substitute for the emotional connection we get from talking face-to-face. It's like having a placeholder for real connection, but it sometimes leaves us wanting more in terms of that sense of belonging we all crave.

Rather than dismiss texting altogether, see it as a useful starting point. It can serve as a spark that leads to deeper interaction. A simple message like "Thinking of you!" or "Let's chat soon" can really pave the way for a deeper connection. It's a friendly nudge that shows you care, and it can lead to more meaningful interactions down the line.

Texting and Social Motivation

When you text, your brain doesn't activate the same reward systems as it does during real-time interactions. It's not that texting is inherently bad. It's incomplete. It can initiate a connection, but it's not designed to sustain it.

- **Mirror Neurons Don't Fire:** Without visual or vocal cues, your brain doesn't get the empathy boost it craves.
- **Oxytocin Is Absent:** No physical presence means no bonding hormone.

- **Delayed Dopamine Release:** The anticipation of a response creates a "waiting game" effect that can heighten anxiety rather than satisfaction.

This texting gap is similar to what happens on social media. You see a friend's post, like it, and maybe leave a comment, thinking you've "connected." These interactions often leave us wanting more. Social media can amplify feelings of loneliness through the illusion of connection. You're technically interacting, but you're not engaging in a meaningful way.

It's no wonder studies show that heavy social media use is linked to increased loneliness and anxiety. Social media also introduces harmful comparisons, where you measure your life against someone else's highlight reel.

Aisha and Priya's Texting Trap

Aisha had been feeling distant from her best friend, Priya. They used to talk for hours on the phone, but lately, their conversations had been reduced to sporadic texts.

One night, after a long day at work, Aisha sent Priya a heartfelt message: "I've been feeling so overwhelmed lately. I miss our talks." Priya replied a few minutes later: "Same here. Let's talk soon!"

While Priya's response was kind, it didn't give Aisha the reassurance she needed. The exchange felt unfinished, leaving Aisha more isolated than before. She realized that texting wasn't solving the problem. It was prolonging it. The next day, Aisha called Priya. Hearing her voice immediately lifted Aisha's mood, and by the end of their conversation, she felt like a weight had been lifted. That moment reminded her of what she'd been missing, not just words, but warmth, energy, and connection.

The difference? Real-time interaction allowed Aisha and Priya to exchange energy, empathy, and laughter. None of which came through in a text.

How to Use Texting as a Bridge, Not a Crutch

Texting can have its place in your communication toolkit, but only if you use it intentionally.

1. **Initiate Real-Time Interaction:** Use texts to set up calls, video chats, or in-person meetups. For example:
   Instead of: "How's it going?"
   Try: "I'd love to catch up! Are you free for a call later this week?"
2. **Avoid Emotional Conversations Over Text:** If you need support or want to discuss something important, pick up the phone. Texting can easily lead to misinterpretation or an unresolved exchange.
3. **Limit Texting for Logistics:** Keep texts short and purposeful for things like scheduling or sharing quick updates.

Texting can create the spark of connection, but it's the in-person or real-time follow-up that fuels the fire. When you shift your communication to focus on presence, you'll find that the connections you're seeking feel deeper, more fulfilling, and ultimately, more human.

Real-time interactions—whether in person, on a video call, or even over the phone—offer offer something that delayed communication like texting can't. They create a feedback loop of connection, where you give and receive energy in the moment.

It's this immediacy that makes real-time connections so powerful.

Virtual tools have their place, but nothing compares to the deep, fulfilling experience of being physically present.

Research shows that the happiest people aren't necessarily the most social or outgoing. They're the ones who consistently make time for meaningful interactions. Whether it's a quick coffee date, a weekly family dinner, or a spontaneous phone call, these moments are like deposits in your happiness bank account.

But what happens when our drive for connection is disrupted? This is where loneliness plays a dangerous role.

Loneliness Suppresses Social Motivation

Here's the tricky part: when loneliness creeps in, it throws this whole reward system out of balance. The very thing that's designed to motivate us to connect—our brain's reward system—starts to work against us.

When we're lonely, our brains shift into survival mode. It's like the system panics and assumes, "Something's wrong here. We're alone, so we must be in danger." This triggers the fight-or-flight response, flooding the body with stress hormones like cortisol.

In small doses, this response is helpful. It keeps us alert to threats and helps us solve problems. But when it becomes chronic, like in long-term loneliness, it hijacks the brain's ability to focus on connection.

Here's why: loneliness suppresses the release of dopamine and oxytocin. Without those "feel-good" chemicals, social interactions lose their emotional payoff. You might find yourself thinking, "What's the point of reaching out? It probably won't help anyway." This lack of reward dampens your motivation to connect, making socializing feel harder, less appealing, or even exhausting. The result? A negative feedback loop where loneliness feeds itself.

Instead of feeling energized by the thought of seeing friends or meeting new people, loneliness makes us feel drained before we even try.

> **SOCIAL BONDING IS WIRED INTO YOUR BRAIN**
>
> Your brain is built for connections and it's key to our survival! Every time you engage in a meaningful social interaction, your brain rewards you with feel-good chemicals like dopamine and oxytocin. It's nature's way of saying, nature's way of saying, *"Keep doing this —it's good for you!"*
>
> **Loneliness throws your brain's reward system out of whack.** Instead of feeling energized by the idea of connecting, you feel drained. Why? Stress hormones like cortisol flood your system, hijacking your ability to bond. This can make reaching out feel like climbing a mountain.
>
> **Quick Fix:** Start small. Smile at someone. Send a text. Science shows even brief interactions can spark the brain's reward system and nudge you back toward connection.

It's why calling a friend or showing up at an event can seem overwhelming when we're feeling isolated. The effort feels greater than the reward, so we pull back even further. Over time, this withdrawal reinforces the cycle, making the reward system even less active and the loneliness even deeper.

Breaking the Cycle

The good news is that this feedback loop isn't permanent. Neuroscience shows that even small, positive social interactions can reignite the brain's reward system. In-person interactions trigger mirror neurons, release oxytocin, and trigger a release of dopamine. But when you've been isolated or out of practice, your brain adapts to solitude, making it harder to muster the energy for connection. It's like exercising a muscle you haven't used—stiff at first, but small, manageable actions can help rebuild its strength. A simple chat with a coworker, a kind word to a neighbor, or even a moment of eye contact with a stranger can begin to restore balance.

By taking intentional steps to reconnect, you can gradually reset your brain's reward system, making connections feel natural and rewarding again. It's not about giant leaps; it's about small, consistent actions that help rebuild your brain's motivation to connect.

Loneliness doesn't just affect the brain. It also warps how we see ourselves and the world. Psychologists refer to this as cognitive distortions, or *thinking errors*. When loneliness takes hold, it amplifies these errors, leading to negative thoughts like, *No one cares about me*, or *I'm just not interesting enough*. Thinking errors are like little mental traps that trick us into seeing things in a skewed, usually negative way. These thoughts create barriers to connection, like self-doubt, fear of rejection, and avoidance behaviors. We'll take a closer look at these thinking errors in future chapters.

Rebuild Your Social Motivation

Research shows that the amount of time we spend physically around other people is a predictor of happiness. It sounds simple, but if you've ever hesitated to reach out to someone or felt drained at the thought of socializing, you know that rebuilding your social motivation can feel daunting at first.

The good news is, you don't need to dive headfirst into big social events to regain that spark. In fact, even small moments of connection—what are sometimes called "micro-doses of belonging"—can be enough to shift your mindset and energize your day.

The Power of Small Connections

If you've ever sat silently on a train, staring out the window or scrolling through your phone, you might have assumed that striking up a conversation with the stranger next to you would be awkward, or worse, unwelcome. Psychologists have tested this assumption. In a series of experiments, they uncovered something surprising: small social connections, even with complete strangers, can bring us more joy than we think.

In one study, they asked Chicago commuters to take a leap of faith. Some were instructed to strike up a conversation with a fellow passenger, while others were asked to keep to themselves. The results were striking: those who chatted with strangers reported feeling happier and more connected than those who stayed in their own bubble. Despite common fears of rejection, most participants found their fellow commuters friendly and willing to engage.

Do you avoid small interactions with strangers because you think this will feel awkward or that you will not enjoy doing this? What if you knew that many studies show a different story? The reality is that even a quick chat with someone can leave you feeling more upbeat and energized than you expect.

Psychologists discovered that it's not just about small talk. Even deeper conversations with strangers create stronger feelings of connection and greater enjoyment. People are usually more open to meaningful connection than we think, and it can lead to something really special.

So why don't we do this more often? Many of us hold back because we fear rejection, worry about bothering someone, or assume that others simply aren't interested. But research shows our fears are often unfounded. In fact, most people are far more receptive to connection than we might believe.

All of this research reveals something important: building happiness and social motivation doesn't always require grand gestures or lifelong friendships. Sometimes, it's as simple as saying hello to the person sitting next to you or turning a brief encounter into something meaningful. These small connections might not seem like much, but their power to uplift and energize us is undeniable.

- **Why They Work:** These small moments are like mini-rehearsals for deeper connection. They activate the same social pathways in your brain, reminding you that interacting with others can be joyful, not exhausting.
- **Immediate Rewards:** A quick chat with a stranger or a kind word to someone you pass on the street can make both of you feel seen, valued, and part of something bigger.

The Ripple Effect of Small Actions

One of the most fascinating findings from psychology research is that the benefits of these small interactions aren't one-sided. When you smile at someone or share a quick conversation, you're not just boosting your own happiness; you're brightening their day too. **Connection is contagious.**

Happiness comes from being around others, even in small ways. Each micro-dose of belonging is a step toward rebuilding the social fabric that grounds us, one tiny thread at a time.

Eddie used to love mornings. He'd grab a coffee at his local diner, chat with the waitress about their shared love of classic rock music, and wave at the other regulars before heading to work. But after the pandemic, those moments faded, leaving Eddie to start his days in silence. Even when the diner reopened, he felt awkward stepping back into those casual interactions.

One morning, he made a small decision: when the waitress asked how his day was going, he didn't just mumble "fine." Instead, he smiled and asked, "How about you?" Her face lit up with surprise and warmth, and they ended up laughing together about the rainy weather. In that simple exchange, something shifted, not just for Eddie but for both of them. He left the diner feeling lighter, more connected to the world around him. And judging by the waitress's smile, she did too. It wasn't a big moment, but it created a small ripple of positivity. Proof that even tiny acts of connection can lift two people at once. Over time, Eddie began to rebuild those small connections, and with each one, his social motivation grew stronger.

Moments like these might seem small, but they have a ripple effect, brightening not just our own day but the day of someone else too.

How to Rebuild Social Motivation

1. **Start with Micro-Doses:** Look for opportunities to engage in small, low-pressure interactions. For example:

- Compliment someone on their outfit.
- Make eye contact and smile at a neighbor.
- Say "thank you" with warmth and intention to a cashier.

These moments take only seconds but can shift your mindset for the rest of the day.

2. **Lower the Stakes:** Not every interaction needs to be deep or life-changing. A quick chat about the weather or a passing joke is enough to activate your social brain.
3. **Reflect on the Impact:** After a small connection, pause and ask yourself: How did this small moment feel? How did the other person respond? This awareness reinforces the value of connection and motivates you to seek it out more often.

Why Socializing Feels Different Post-Pandemic

Many people find themselves socially drained more quickly than before. It's not a personality change; it's an adaptation to a long period of solitude. And the good news? Adaptations can be reversed.

Why does saying 'yes' to an invitation feel harder than it used to?

It's a question you may have asked yourself recently, staring at a text from a friend or a calendar notification for an event. You want to go. You love the people inviting you. But somehow, staying home feels easier. You're not lazy or antisocial. You're just navigating something millions of others feel too.

The COVID-19 Pandemic of 2020 didn't just disrupt our routines; it rewired our energy and social instincts. For months, socializing wasn't just discouraged. It felt unsafe. Our brains adapted, tipping toward solitude for survival. Without regular social interactions, the "muscles" we once relied on to navigate relationships grew weaker, leaving many of us hesitant to step back into social life.

If you're feeling disconnected or overwhelmed by the thought of reconnecting, know this: it's not a flaw in you. Your brain is simply recalibrating after an extended period of isolation. With small steps and intentional choices, you can rebuild your social confidence and rediscover the joy of connection.

Before the pandemic, social interactions were part of the background hum of life. Small moments like a chat with a coworker, a hug from a friend, or a smile from a stranger weren't just pleasant; they were essential. These interactions acted like the connective tissue of our emotional well-being, balancing our energy and keeping us grounded.

Then, almost overnight, everything changed. It turns out our brains are wired for **social homeostasis**—a natural balance between connection and solitude. The pandemic tipped this balance toward solitude, rewiring our reward systems. Social interactions, once effortless, began to feel draining.

Without regular exposure to these moments, our brains adjusted to a new baseline of solitude, making it harder to reconnect.

Before the pandemic, Jess was the life of every happy hour, thriving on connection. But as months of isolation turned into years, Jess grew comfortable with quiet nights at home. When her best friend Laura invited her to dinner after restrictions eased, Jess hesitated. The thought of conversation felt exhausting, even though she missed her friend.

When Jess finally said yes, she was surprised by the outcome. She started the evening listening more than talking, letting Laura's warmth ease her back into the flow of connection. By the end of dinner, Jess felt lighter, as though a part of herself had woken up again.

The simple joy of laughter and connection reminded her that she hadn't lost her ability to connect. She had just needed the right moment to spark it again.

The truth is, reconnecting takes effort because your brain is out of practice, but it's also deeply rewarding. With each interaction, you're retraining your brain to find joy in connection.

Social interactions aren't only about words. They're about energy. When you're with someone upbeat and positive, their vibe lifts you, creating a sense of connection and ease.

On the flip side, spending time with someone who is stressed or negative can leave you feeling drained. This dynamic, known as **social contagion**, explains why some social environments feel uplifting while others feel exhausting.

Post-pandemic, this energy exchange feels more intense. With social "muscles" out of practice, your tolerance for high-energy or draining interactions might have shifted. Rebuilding your confidence starts with recognizing the energy you bring and the energy you absorb.

Congratulations! You're ready to take the plunge and spend some time with others, and that's awesome! I want this experience to be truly special for you, so let's talk about how to spot those positive social environments out there. You don't have to get it perfect. Just noticing where you feel safe, supported, and light is a wonderful place to begin.

Not every social setting feels the same, but the best ones have some wonderful qualities in common:

- **Mutual Support:** People listen, validate, and encourage one another.
- **Laughter and Lightness:** There's room for humor and playfulness, even during serious moments.
- **Genuine Interest:** Everyone feels seen and valued, without judgment or competition.

Writing this chapter was a revelation. It opened my eyes to the fascinating science behind connection and what truly drives happiness. Our ability to bond with others isn't just emotional; it's rooted in our biology. When we spend time with people, our brain lights up. Connection fuels motivation, boosts our mood, and reinforces the desire to do it again.

Social motivation is like a cycle: the more meaningful interactions we have, the easier it becomes to connect, and the more joy we feel. On the other hand, isolation weakens that cycle, making it harder to reach out even when we want to. But that cycle can be rebuilt.

You don't need to overhaul your social life overnight. One heartfelt conversation can do more for your well-being than hours of distracted scrolling. Connection doesn't mean being "on" all the time; it means being present when it counts. And if you've felt disconnected, know this: even the smallest gestures like a smile, a shared laugh, or a genuine "How are you?" can begin rewiring your brain for connection. Like any muscle, it gets stronger the more you use it.

Connection isn't a luxury; it's essential. It's the lifeline your brain and body need to feel safe, supported, and whole. And when you understand that, connection becomes something to prioritize, not something to wait for.

What This Means: When you engage with others, your brain rewards you with feel-good chemicals like dopamine and oxytocin. Those moments of closeness actually reshape your mood, energy, and motivation.

Why It Matters: Even brief in-person interactions can boost happiness and emotional resilience. Real-time presence—sharing space, laughter, or even silence—activates your body's natural systems for well-being in ways that texts or social media can't.

What Comes Next: Prioritize one meaningful connection this week. It doesn't have to be big, just real. A phone call, a lunch date, a short walk with someone you enjoy. These micro-moments don't just feel good, they rewire your system to seek more of them.

Because at the end of the day,
happiness isn't about what you have.
It's about who you share it with. 🖤

Part 2

Building Internal Confidence

How You Experience the World

You carry your atmosphere with you.

Chapter 5

The Confidence to Be You

"By being yourself, you put something wonderful in the world that was not there before."

— Edwin Elliot

It was my daughter's 10th birthday, and she knew exactly how she wanted to celebrate: dinner at her favorite sushi restaurant with five of her closest friends. These girls, ranging in age from 9 to 11, didn't all hang out together on a regular basis. Different grades, different friend groups, different routines. But every year, they came together for this tradition. And the second they piled into the car, it was like no time had passed.

Talk about **interpersonal synchrony**—their energy was instantly in sync. Even before we left the driveway, the conversation was flying—catching up, debating details of their stories, talking over each other but somehow never missing a beat. The excitement was contagious, filling every inch of our oversized SUV as we started the 35-minute drive to the restaurant.

Then suddenly, in perfect unison: "Turn the music up!"

And just like that, the car turned into a full-blown concert. For the entire ride there and back, they sang at the top of their lungs, completely lost in the moment. Dynamite by Taio Cruz. TikTok by Kesha. Roar by Katy Perry. Every lyric (or at least their version of it) was belted out with confidence. No second-guessing, no worrying about how they sounded, no holding back. Just pure, unfiltered joy.

That moment was social confidence in its truest form. **No one was trying to fit in—they just belonged.** Not because they were the same, but because they showed up fully as themselves, without hesitation, without needing to prove anything. Their connection wasn't about perfection or control. It was about being real. And that's what made them feel so at ease.

DEFINITION

Social Confidence
Trusting that you belong, just by being yourself, and without needing to prove it.

That kind of confidence—the ability to be yourself without overthinking—often gets harder to hold onto as we grow older. Somewhere along the way, we start questioning ourselves:

> *Did I say the right thing?*
> *Was I too much—or not enough?*
> *Do I really belong here?*

Little by little, we learn to second-guess and shrink ourselves, but here's the truth: confidence isn't about being perfect, impressive, or fearless. It's about knowing who you are, that you are enough, and allowing that to guide how you show up in the world. When you stop filtering yourself—stop measuring, adjusting, or performing—you give others permission to do the same. Connection thrives when you are real, not rehearsed.

Before we dive deeper, take a moment to reflect: When was the last time you felt truly in sync with the people around you? A moment when you weren't filtering yourself, second-guessing, or trying to perform? Just fully present, fully you?

Why Confidence Feels Hard

Many people believe that confidence means always feeling sure of yourself, never experiencing doubts, and being outgoing and bold. Time to clear this up: that's just a myth!

If confidence meant we never felt unsure, always knew what to do, or had to be the life of the party, then most of us would be left in the dust. It's no wonder we often feel like confidence is something we can't quite grasp!

The good news is that real confidence is something different altogether. To build it, we first need to let go of those common misconceptions we've picked up along the way. Let's embrace a more realistic and friendly view of what it means to be confident!

Myth #1: Confident People Never Feel Insecure

Reality: Even the most self-assured people experience doubt. They just don't let it stop them. Confidence isn't the absence of fear; it's the willingness to act despite it.

Think about a time when you gave a presentation at work or school. Maybe your hands shook a little. Maybe your heart raced. But you stood up and spoke anyway.

That was confidence, not because you felt fearless, but because you showed up despite the nerves. True confidence isn't about always feeling certain. It's about believing in yourself enough to move forward even when you don't.

Myth #2: Confidence Means Being Extroverted and Charismatic

Reality: Confidence isn't about being the center of attention or having a big personality. Quiet, introspective people can be just as confident because confidence is about knowing who you are and trusting yourself.

Picture someone who doesn't say a lot in a group conversation, but when they do, people listen. They're steady, calm, and sure of themselves. Not because they're dominating the room, but because they're grounded in who they are.

Confidence isn't about performing for others. It's about using your voice and your presence, whether you're speaking loudly or softly.

Myth #3: Means Never Failing

Reality: The most confident people have failed over and over again. It's important to remember that true confidence isn't about avoiding mistakes. It's all about the valuable lessons we gain when things don't go as we hoped.

Think back to a time when you tried something new, whether it was learning a skill, applying for a job, or putting yourself out there socially. Maybe it didn't go perfectly. Maybe you got rejected or had an awkward moment. But if you reflected, learned, and tried again, that was confidence in action.

Confidence isn't built by avoiding failure. It's built by getting back up after the fall.

When we let go of those myths, confidence can truly be within reach. You don't have to be perfect, fearless, or always outgoing. Instead, focus on being yourself and believing that you have so much to offer, even on those days when you're feeling unsure.

It's easy to feel confident when everything is going smoothly. But what about those high-pressure situations that make your heart race, your mind second-guess, or your voice catch in your throat? Those moments when you need it most?

Real confidence isn't just something you have, it's something you prepare for. Let's look at simple ways to prepare for challenges. When tough situations show up, you won't be caught off guard. You'll have the tools to trust yourself, even when things get difficult.

Preparing for Confidence in Hard Situations

Confidence isn't just about how you feel in everyday moments. It's about how you show up when it matters most.

We've all been there:

- A high-pressure situation where you freeze instead of speaking up.
- A tough conversation you know you need to have, but keep avoiding.
- A social event where you feel out of place and unsure of what to say.

It's easy to think that we should just naturally have confidence in those moments. Real confidence isn't magic. It's something we can build and prepare for. Leadership expert Ritu Bhasin, in her work on authenticity and belonging, outlines a powerful five-step approach for facing these challenges with more courage. Using her ideas as inspiration, we'll walk through how you can apply them in real life.

Let's look at how Joe, a video game designer, could use these strategies to navigate a tough social situation at work.

Joe's Story: Feeling Overlooked and Hurt at Work

Joe has been working at his game development studio for two years. In his office, it's common for birthday cards to go around for everyone to sign, followed by cake in the break room. The first year, Joe's birthday passed without notice. He figured it was because he was new. But the next year, the same thing happened. A week later, during a team meeting, a coworker asked everyone to chip in for a new employee's birthday cake.

Joe sat in silence, feeling hurt and overlooked. He didn't know what to do. Should he speak up? Should he give money for the cake, even though no one celebrated his birthday? Or should he just start looking for a new job? It would have been easy for Joe to sit in resentment.

Instead of sitting in resentment, Joe could prepare himself for situations like this by using five key strategies.

STEP 1: SCRIPTING – PLAN WHAT YOU'LL SAY IN ADVANCE

Have you ever walked away from a conversation and immediately thought of the perfect thing you should have said? That's because, in stressful moments, our brains can struggle to come up with the right words. Confidence doesn't mean thinking on the spot. It means being prepared.

How Joe Can Use Scripting:

Joe knows that if birthdays keep getting acknowledged in the office, but not his, this will continue to bother him. Instead of hoping it won't happen again, **he can prepare what to say in advance.** He might decide that, next time a coworker brings up birthday celebrations, he'll say something like:

"Hey, I noticed we do birthday celebrations in the office, but mine was missed the past two years. I'd love to be included in the future."

Instead of holding onto resentment, this gives him a clear, direct way to communicate his feelings before the moment catches him off guard.

☞ **TRY THIS:**

Prepare yourself with a few powerful phrases you can use in real life. Think about situations that have left you feeling frozen, overlooked, or unsure of what to say. Then, choose a few phrases you can keep in your back pocket, ready for when you need them. Here are some examples:

In a high-pressure or disrespectful situation:
(workplace, classroom, social group)

- "I'm confident in what I shared. I'd appreciate it if we could stick to the facts."
- "I'm not comfortable with how this conversation is going. Let's revisit it when we can talk respectfully."
- "I understand you see it differently. Here's my perspective."

When someone says something hurtful or dismissive:
(friend group, casual setting)

- "When you said that, it made me feel left out. I just wanted to be honest about how it landed for me."
- "I value our friendship, which is why I wanted to bring this up instead of holding it inside."

As a bystander witnessing bullying or disrespect:

- "Hey, that's not okay. Let's keep it respectful."
- "Are you alright? You don't deserve to be spoken to like that."

- "Let's take a breath. No one here deserves to be treated that way."

When you need to exit or pause a tense situation:
- "I'm stepping away to collect my thoughts."
- "This conversation isn't constructive for me right now."
- "I'll respond later when I've had time to think."

Remember: You don't have to say the "perfect" thing. You just have to protect your peace.

STEP 2: CHOOSE A MANTRA OR AFFIRMATION FOR WHEN DOUBT CREEPS IN

Even when you've prepared what to say, self-doubt can still sneak in. That's where affirmations or mantras come in. They help redirect your thoughts in the moment.

How Joe Can Use an Affirmation:

Let's say Joe starts second-guessing himself:
- *What if people think I'm being dramatic?*
- *What if I make things awkward?*
- *Maybe I should just let it go.*

Instead of spiraling, Joe can ground himself with a simple affirmation like:

"My feelings are valid, and I deserve to be included."

This reminds him of his worth and helps him move past the fear of speaking up.

☞ **TRY THIS:**

Create a few powerful mantras or affirmations to ground yourself when self-doubt tries to take over. When negative thoughts creep in, it's easy to spiral. Having a personal mantra ready gives your brain a quick, positive script to follow instead. Here are some examples:

If you start second-guessing yourself:
- "I trust myself to handle this moment."
- "I belong here. My presence matters."
- "I am more capable than I feel right now."

If you worry about being judged:
- "Their opinions don't define my worth."
- "I don't need to be perfect to be respected."
- "Showing up as myself is more important than impressing others."

If you feel like shrinking or hiding:
- "I am allowed to take up space."
- "My voice is strong. My feelings are valid."
- "It's safe for me to be seen and heard."

Bonus tip: Write your favorite mantra on a sticky note or save it as a phone lock screen.

Remember: The more you repeat it, the easier it becomes to override those old self-doubt scripts.

STEP 3: CALMING THE BODY

Confidence isn't just in your mind; it's in your body too. When we feel nervous, our bodies react:
- Racing heartbeat
- Shaky hands
- Tight shoulders

Instead of trying to think your way into confidence, learn to calm your body first.

How Joe Can Use Calming Techniques:

Joe knows that if he brings this up in a future conversation, he'll probably feel nervous. Instead of letting that overwhelm him, he can prepare by:
- **Taking slow, deep breaths** before the conversation to relax his body.
- **Rolling his shoulders back** to release tension.
- **Standing tall instead of shrinking into himself** (because posture affects confidence!).

By practicing these small physical resets, he signals to his brain: **"I am safe. I am in control."**

☞ TRY THIS:

Practice a few quick ways to calm your body when anxiety starts to take over. When your nervous system is activated, it's easy to feel trapped in panic or tension. Small physical shifts can send powerful signals to your brain that you're safe and help you regain control in real time. Here are a few techniques you can try anytime:

If your heart is racing or you feel shaky:
- Box Breathing: Inhale for 4 counts, hold for 4 counts, exhale for 4 counts, hold for 4 counts. Repeat.

  (Tip: Imagine drawing a square with your breath.)

If you feel tense and closed off:
- Ground Your Body: Plant your feet firmly on the floor. Relax your shoulders.

  (Tip: Imagine roots growing from your feet into the ground beneath you.)

If your voice feels tight or shaky:
- Release Tension with Movement: Gently roll your shoulders back and down. Stretch your neck side to side. Loosen your jaw.

Remember: Your body isn't working against you. It's trying to protect you. Calming your body calms your mind.

STEP 4: VISUALIZATION – MENTALLY REHEARSE SUCCESS

Elite athletes, performers, and speakers all use visualization to prepare for high-stakes moments. Why? **Because your brain doesn't know the difference between real and imagined experiences.** By picturing yourself succeeding, you're training your mind to believe in that outcome.

How Joe Can Use Visualization:

Instead of worrying about the conversation going badly, Joe can imagine it going well.
- He can visualize himself speaking up with confidence and his coworkers responding positively.

- He can picture the conversation flowing smoothly instead of awkwardly.
- He can see himself walking away feeling proud, knowing he advocated for himself.

This simple mental rehearsal lowers anxiety and helps him feel more prepared.

☞ **TRY THIS:**

Prepare your mind like an athlete prepares for a big game. Choose an upcoming situation where you want to feel more confident: a meeting, a tough conversation, or a social event. Spend 2–3 minutes quietly picturing yourself:

- Speaking clearly and calmly.
- Staying grounded even if you feel nervous.
- Handling any awkward moments with ease and grace.
- Walking away feeling proud of how you showed up.

Remember: Even a few minutes of positive rehearsal can create new pathways in your brain for confidence.

STEP 5: ANCHOR YOURSELF IN YOUR "WHY"

When you're about to face a tough situation, it's easy to get caught up in anxiety or second-guessing. But if you take a moment to anchor yourself in why this conversation or action matters to you, it can shift your energy from fear to purpose.

Instead of focusing on what could go wrong, you ground yourself in what you stand for, like respect, inclusion, or self-worth. Remembering your "why" helps you act with intention, even when it's uncomfortable.

How Joe Can Use Anchoring:

Joe knows that birthday celebrations at work may seem small, but being seen and valued by his team is important to him. Before speaking up, he reminds himself:
- "I deserve to feel included, just like everyone else."
- "Respect and fairness matter; it's okay to ask for it."

By connecting to these personal values, Joe strengthens his confidence. He isn't speaking up just for the sake of it. He's honoring what's important to him. This makes it easier to move through fear and have a direct, respectful conversation.

☞ **TRY THIS:**

Before a challenging moment, take one minute to reflect on your "why." Ask yourself:
- Why does speaking up matter to me?
- What value am I standing for?

Write it down or repeat it to yourself as a grounding reminder. When you act from your "why," you carry your confidence with you, no matter how others respond.

Confidence grows
when you stand for something
that matters to you.

Confidence Is a Skill You Can Build

Most people think confidence is something you either have or don't. But the truth is, confidence is a skill you can train.

- ✔ Scripting helps you prepare your words.
- ✔ Affirmations help you reframe self-doubt.
- ✔ Calming techniques regulate your nervous system.
- ✔ Visualization primes your brain for success.
- ✔ Anchor yourself to remember your "why."

The next time you're facing a challenging situation, don't just hope for confidence—prepare for it.

WHAT IF THE FIRST THING THEY SEE ISN'T YOU?

Some people enter a room and feel invisible. Others feel like they're on display. If that's you, if you've ever felt like the first thing people notice is your wheelchair, your body, your difference, I want to say: I see you.

It's exhausting to feel like you have to explain yourself before you even say hello. To wonder if people are seeing you, or just the label they've attached to you. But here's the truth: **you don't have to earn the right to belong.**

The people who are meant to connect with you—the real you—will feel your energy, your heart, your presence. That's what connection is built on. Not perfection. Not appearances. Just presence and truth. Confidence doesn't come from pretending you're not different. It comes from owning the energy you carry and trusting that it's enough.

You deserve friendships that start with curiosity, not assumptions. Spaces where your whole self is welcome. You are not too much, and you are not too different.

You are already worthy of being known, exactly as you are.

The Role of Balanced Energy in Authenticity

Authentic confidence doesn't come from trying to fit into a mold. It comes from being aligned with yourself. This is where balanced energy comes in. As discussed in Chapter 2, balanced energy is about creating harmony between how you feel on the inside and how you present yourself on the outside. When your internal and external energy match, you naturally project confidence effortlessly, without needing to fake it.

INSIDE: Trusting Yourself Enough to Show Up as You

This is the foundation of confidence. It's about knowing who you are, what you value, and believing that you are enough. Think of someone who has internal confidence. They don't seek approval, they don't over-explain themselves, and they don't shrink to make others comfortable. They show up as they are, and that's what makes them magnetic.

- They trust their opinions.
- They don't need constant validation.
- They carry themselves with certainty, even when they don't have all the answers.

Ask yourself: Where do I feel the most like myself? How can I bring that energy into other areas of my life?

OUTSIDE: People Trust You and Want to Be Around You

When you trust yourself on the inside, people naturally pick up on that energy. You don't need to convince others you're confident. They can feel it. When you are comfortable in your own skin, others sense it and respond.

- You communicate with ease.
- You create an inviting presence.
- People feel drawn to your energy, not because you're "perfect" but because you're real.

The next time you walk into a room, instead of thinking *how can I impress people?* Shift your mindset to *how can I show up as my true self?*

Practice Balanced Energy in Your Life

Bringing balanced energy into your daily life starts with small shifts. Do I shrink myself in certain spaces to avoid attention? Do I force myself to be more outgoing than I naturally am? Do I change my personality depending on who I'm around?

Confidence comes from consistency. When your inner and outer energy match, you feel most at ease.

If you're naturally introverted, own that. You don't have to be outgoing to be confident. If you're naturally expressive, embrace it without worrying about being "too much."

Confidence doesn't always come from thinking. It often comes from how you feel in your body. Take a deep breath before speaking in a group setting to calm your nervous system. Keep your posture open instead of folding inward. Slow your speech; rushing your words can make you feel less in control.

When you trust yourself, you don't justify your choices.

- Say what you mean, then stop.
- Let your words sit without rushing to fill silence.
- Trust that your voice is enough.

What This Means: Confidence is about becoming comfortable with yourself (not proving yourself to others). When you stop filtering everything through *Will they accept me?* and instead ask, *Am I being real right now?* you start to feel free.

Why It Matters: When you trust yourself, you move through the world with more ease. You speak up more. You reach out more. You connect more. Confidence isn't the absence of fear. It's the presence of self-belief. And the only way to build it is by practicing honesty with yourself, one moment at a time.

What Comes Next: Notice one moment today where you held back, minimized yourself, or questioned your worth. What might you say or do differently next time? Confidence grows through small experiments in self-expression. Let the next one be yours.

When you start believing in yourself, the world can't help but do the same. And it all starts with you. 🖤

> *"To be yourself in a world that is constantly trying to make you something else is the greatest accomplishment."*
>
> – Ralph Waldo Emerson

Chapter 6

Stop Being So Hard on Yourself

"I am the greatest. I said that even before I knew I was."

— Muhammad Ali

You know, I've got this amazing friend named Joy (fitting name, right?), and I just have to share how incredible she is. Whenever someone is going through a tough time, she's the first person they turn to. It's like she always knows just what to say. I can hear her now: "You've got this! You're doing your best, and remember, one mistake doesn't define you!" It's so comforting. Honestly, being around her just lifts your spirits!

Don't you just love having friends like that? She has this unique ability to make people feel truly seen, valued, and worthy. But when it comes to herself, it's a different story.

Maybe you know someone like this?

Or maybe this is you?

One evening, Joy found herself just staring at her computer, trying to finish an email to her boss, but she was totally stuck. She couldn't stop thinking about what happened earlier that day. She had spoken up in a meeting, and honestly, it didn't go at all like she had hoped. Now, her mind was just stuck on replay, going over that moment again and again, tearing herself apart for it. It's like those little regrets just refuse to let go.

"That was so embarrassing. Why did I even say that? Everyone probably thinks I don't know what I'm doing. What if they think I'm not cut out for this?" As she re-read the email draft, another thought hit her: What if I sound stupid in this, too? She deleted everything and closed her laptop. "I'm just too exhausted to deal with this right now."

Later that night, she called me, her voice unusually quiet. "I don't get it," she admitted. "If you had been in that meeting and said the exact same thing, I would've told you it wasn't a big deal. I would've reminded you of all the times you did say the right thing. So why can't I do that for myself?"

And she was right.

I reminded her of something I read once:

"If we spoke to our friends
the way we speak to ourselves,
we wouldn't have any friends left."

That realization hit her hard.

So, I suggested an experiment: What if you talked to yourself the way you talk to Sam? (Sam is Joy's younger brother, and the person she's most protective of.)

The next morning, she decided to give it a try. When self-doubt crept in, she caught herself. Instead of thinking, *You're so stupid,* she tried, *Okay, yesterday wasn't perfect, but I'm learning. And one moment doesn't erase all the good things I've done.* It wasn't magic. It didn't erase her doubts overnight. But it was a start.

And that one small shift? It changed everything.

We spend so much time focusing on external relationships—our friends, our partners, our colleagues—but what about the relationship that runs the deepest? The one that's with you every single day, in every single moment?

Your relationship with yourself.

Think about it: You are the one person you spend the most time with. How you talk to yourself, judge yourself, and show up for yourself affects everything. It shapes how you carry yourself in conversations, how you handle setbacks, how you take risks, and how you allow others to treat you.

So why are most of us kinder to other people than we are to ourselves? I bet that you comfort your friends when they're down. You reassure them when they doubt themselves. And you probably remind them of all their qualities. But when it comes to yourself, you sound more like a harsh critic than a supportive friend. The good news? This can change.

> Self-compassion isn't just about "being nice" to ourselves—it's a skill. One that we can practice, strengthen, and use to transform our confidence, our resilience, and our happiness.

Self-compassion is important because:
- If you want stronger relationships, you have to start with the one you have with yourself.
- How you talk to yourself affects how you show up in the world.
- And when you start treating yourself with the same kindness you give others, everything shifts.

This chapter is about rewiring that inner dialogue. About catching the voice that says, "I'm not good enough," and challenging it. It's about replacing criticism with compassion.

Because the strongest connections don't start with what's outside, they start with what's inside.

Why does self-criticism come so naturally? (Hint: it's not your fault—it's how your brain is wired.) You're about to get the answer to this question and also learn why self-compassion is one of the most powerful tools you can develop.

But for now, here's a question to sit with: If we spoke to our friends the way we speak to ourselves, we wouldn't have any friends left.

Why We're So Hard on Ourselves

Have you ever noticed that you can receive ten compliments, but one single piece of criticism stays with you for days? You replay it in your mind, obsess over it, and somehow, it holds more weight than all the positive things people have said. That's not just you being overly sensitive. It's your brain's natural wiring.

The Built-In Negativity Bias

Your brain's main job isn't to make you happy—it's to keep you alive. When I first heard that, it honestly surprised me. I'd assumed happiness was part of the deal. But your brain is wired for survival, not satisfaction. It constantly scans for threats, processes information fast, and conserves energy whenever possible.

Efficiency is a big part of that. If something doesn't help you stay safe or navigate the world, your brain doesn't want to spend energy on it. Feeling good is nice, but it's more of a bonus than the point.

For our ancestors, survival meant staying alert to anything that could go wrong: predators, spoiled food, even social rejection. The ones who stayed hyper-aware lived longer, and we inherited that wiring.

Today, we aren't running from wild animals, but our brains still treat modern stress like danger. A mistake at work, an awkward silence, a text left on read—it all sets off that same internal alarm.

This is what psychologists call **negativity bias**: our brain's tendency to focus more on what's wrong than what's going well.

Here's how it plays out in different areas of life:

- **One mistake outweighs a dozen successes.** You could do everything right, give a solid presentation at work, get praised by your professor, or even have a great time at a party. But if you stumble over your words in a meeting or forget an important email, that's what your mind replays on a loop.
- **Pain sticks, pleasure fades.** Science shows that negative experiences create stronger memories than positive ones, which is why you keep replaying that embarrassing moment from last week, but barely remember the compliment someone gave you.
- **Self-doubt feels like a safety net.** But one made of barbed wire. It promises to catch you, but mostly just keeps you tangled up. Your brain convinces you that you'll be prepared for the worst if you overthink every possible mistake. But instead of helping, it just keeps you stuck in a cycle of stress and second-guessing.

DEFINITION

Negativity Bias

The brain's tendency to focus more on negative experiences, emotions, and information than positive ones.

Maybe you second-guess texting first after a great date because you don't want to seem too eager. Your brain convinces you that anticipating rejection or failure will somehow soften the impact, when in reality, it just keeps you from fully engaging in life.

So here is the problem: What helped our ancestors survive the wild doesn't really help us thrive in everyday life today. Instead of keeping us safe, this negativity bias just holds us back.

Negativity bias, when left unchecked, increases self-doubt, anxiety, and self-criticism, convincing us that we're not good enough, smart enough, or capable enough. And that leads us to a bigger problem: your inner critic.

Your Inner Critic

Have you ever stopped to think about how you talk to yourself? It's interesting, right? We all have this inner voice chatting away in our heads throughout the day. Unfortunately, that voice isn't particularly friendly or encouraging. Instead of lifting us up, it often sounds like:

- *I'm not good enough.*
- *I always mess up.*
- *I don't deserve happiness.*
- *What's wrong with me?*
- *I'll never get this right.*

The worst part is that we don't even question these thoughts. We just believe they are true, as if they're facts. *Wow, you're such a failure. You always screw up. You don't deserve good things.* If someone said these things to your friend, you'd be ready to defend them, wouldn't you? You wouldn't let anyone treat them that way!

So, why do we do this to ourselves? **We fall into this trap because we've been conditioned to believe that self-criticism is necessary for improvement.** That being "hard on ourselves" is how we grow, stay motivated, and push through challenges.

Your inner critic means well. Its goal is to protect you from embarrassment, rejection, and failure. It wants to keep you in check so you don't make a fool of yourself. But here's the problem. It's terrible at its job. When self-criticism goes too far, it doesn't motivate—it paralyzes.

The irony of self-criticism:
We think being hard on ourselves will push us to be better, but research shows that
self-criticism actually lowers motivation.

Here's why:
- **It triggers stress, not growth.** When we attack ourselves, our brain registers this as danger and releases stress hormones like cortisol. Instead of motivating us, it's like a fire alarm that goes off at the slightest spark, even when there's no real danger.
- **It creates a fear of failure.** If every mistake leads to harsh self-judgment, we start avoiding challenges altogether. We

procrastinate, shrink back, or don't try at all because failure feels too painful.
- **It reinforces negative identity beliefs.** When we constantly tell ourselves, "I'm such a failure" or "I'll never get this right", our brain starts to believe it. And when we believe something about ourselves, we subconsciously act in ways that reinforce that belief.

So if self-criticism doesn't work, what does?

How Self-Compassion Changes Your Brain

If you've ever thought, *I just need to be tougher on myself so I'll do better,* you're not alone. We've been taught that being self-critical helps us stay accountable, stay motivated, and improve. It turns out that self-compassion, rather than self-judgment, is what truly supports our growth.

Self-compassion isn't about ignoring your mistakes or making excuses. It's about giving yourself the same respect you'd give a friend. Studies show that **people who practice self-compassion are actually more motivated, more resilient, and less likely to give up after failure.**

Researchers on self-compassion have spent decades investigating what happens when people shift from self-criticism to self-kindness. The discoveries are eye-opening!

1. **Self-compassion reduces stress and anxiety.**
    - When we're self-critical, our brain perceives it as an attack, even though it's coming from ourselves.
    - This triggers the fight-or-flight response, flooding our system with cortisol (the stress hormone).

- Over time, chronic self-judgment keeps us in a state of stress, which weakens our ability to cope with challenges.
- But when we practice self-compassion, our soothing system kicks in, reducing cortisol and calming the nervous system.

2. **Self-compassion increases resilience and motivation.**
   - Contrary to popular belief, being kind to yourself doesn't make you lazy. It makes you more likely to bounce back after failure.
   - People who practice self-compassion are more motivated to improve because they aren't afraid of failure.
   - Studies show that when we forgive ourselves for mistakes, we're actually more likely to try again instead of shutting down.

3. **Self-compassion strengthens emotional regulation.**
   - The more we practice self-kindness, the stronger our prefrontal cortex (the brain's rational, problem-solving center) becomes.
   - This means we're better able to pause, reflect, and respond to challenges instead of reacting impulsively.

4. **It boosts oxytocin, the "love hormone."**
   - Self-compassion activates the same bonding system that makes us feel connected to others, creates feelings of warmth, trust, and security.
   - Oxytocin evolved to help us feel bonded and safe in our tribe. When we show ourselves compassion, we tap into that same ancient system.

- Essentially, self-compassion tells our brain: I am safe. I am supported. I am enough.

Self-Criticism vs. Self-Compassion

Let's break this down into two scenarios:

Self-Criticism Cycle:
1. You make a mistake.
2. Your inner critic immediately attacks:
   I'm so stupid. I always mess things up.
3. Your brain perceives this as a threat
   → Triggers fight-or-flight response → Increases stress.
4. Instead of learning from the mistake, you spiral into self-doubt, avoidance, or overcompensating.
5. Keeps you stuck in survival mode.

Self-Compassion Cycle:
1. You make a mistake.
2. Your self-kindness kicks in:
   That was tough, but I'm human. What can I learn from this?
3. Your brain feels safe
   → Triggers oxytocin release
   → Encourages problem-solving and resilience.
4. You process the mistake in a way that helps search for a solution instead of shutting down.
5. Moves you into growth mode.

See the difference?

One keeps you stuck in fear. The other keeps you moving toward growth.

The good news is that self-compassion is a skill that can be developed through practice. Just like exercising in the gym strengthens your muscles, practicing self-kindness enhances your self-compassion circuits, making it easier to respond to setbacks with resilience rather than self-judgment. Since self-compassion is essential for breaking the cycle of self-criticism, how can we learn to practice it? The first step is to stop negative self-talk, and then we can break down the steps to bring more self-compassion into our lives.

How to Change Negative Self-Talk

We all have that voice in our head. The one that whispers: *you're not good enough, you always mess up, why can't you just get it together?*

For most of us, this negative self-talk feels automatic, like it's just how our brain works. But here's something you might not realize: Your brain isn't trying to be cruel. It's just trying to be efficient. Let's break down why our brain creates negative thought patterns and, more importantly, how we can rewrite them.

DEFINITION

Cognitive Distortions (Thinking Errors)
Mental shortcuts that can trick you into seeing the world in a more negative way than it really is.

Your brain is built to make sense of the world fast. It processes an overwhelming amount of information every second, so instead of analyzing every detail carefully, it takes shortcuts—quick mental rules that help you decide what's important.

These shortcuts are known as **cognitive distortions**, patterns of thinking that simplify reality but often get it wrong. Let's just call these thinking errors. **These thoughts *feel* real, but they're not facts;** they're mental shortcuts. And once we recognize them for what they are, we can start changing them.

FEELINGS ARE NOT FACTS
A common thinking error is called emotional reasoning. This is when you take your feelings as proof of the truth, believing that if you feel a certain way, it must be true. "I feel nervous around new people, so they must not like me."

"Stop jumping to conclusions." I never found it helpful when someone would say this. However, it now makes sense because I understand the thinking error. **Jumping to conclusions** includes two common traps that act like superpowers: mind reading and fortune telling (predicting the future).

Mind Reading. Don't you hate it when other people tell you what you are thinking? Be careful, this is a really easy mistake we can all make. Mind reading is the thinking error where we assume we know what others are thinking about us, and it's almost always negative. When you're lonely, you're more likely to think: *they didn't ask how I was doing, so they must not care about me,* forgetting that people might be distracted or overwhelmed themselves. *They canceled our plans because they don't like me,* assuming they don't enjoy your company, and this is a sign of rejection.

Fortune Telling. Wouldn't it be great if we could actually predict the future? That would make things so much easier. This is a common mental shortcut where you predict things will turn out badly. *No one is going to talk to me at the party, so I might as well not even go,* predicting social failure before even attending. *If I go, people will make fun of me,* expecting rejection without giving people a chance. *If I go on a date, it'll probably be a disaster,* again, assuming failure before it even happens.

Here's how your brain's negativity bias (for survival) and mental shortcuts (for efficiency) are tricking you:

You: They didn't ask how I was doing.
Brain: Scanning for what could go wrong + mental shortcut
= That's because they don't care about me.

Or, you can challenge thought:

You: *Hang on... am I mind reading?*
Just because I feel hurt or disappointed doesn't mean I can read their mind.

Noticing these thinking errors is a huge step in flipping the script on them. When you start to recognize these patterns, you begin to understand that they're just distorted perceptions, and definitely not the truth. Every time you catch yourself slipping into a thinking error, you weaken its grip on you and make room for more balanced, positive thoughts.

Thinking errors can be difficult to see in the moment, and like anything else, take practice to identify. The goal is to spot these when you find yourself in a pattern of negative self-talk, so you can then challenge the thought to see if it's really true.

10 Thinking Errors That Fuel Self-Doubt

Here are ten of the most common mental traps we fall into and how to reframe them.

THINKING ERROR	TRAP	REFRAME IT
Feelings Are Not Facts (Emotional Reasoning) Believing that your emotions reflect absolute reality.	*I feel like nobody likes me, so it must be true.*	*Feelings are not facts. Just because I feel lonely doesn't mean people don't care about me.*
Catastrophizing Expecting the absolute worst outcome.	*What if I try to make new friends and they all reject me? I'll always be alone.*	*What if I meet someone who enjoys my company? Not everyone will click, but that doesn't mean I'll always be alone.*
Overgeneralization Assuming that because something bad happened once, it will always happen.	*I always mess up social interactions. No one ever wants to talk to me.*	*That one interaction was awkward, but that doesn't mean I always mess up.*

THINKING ERROR	💬 TRAP	♥ REFRAME IT
Mind Reading Assuming you know what others are thinking, usually something negative.	They haven't responded to my text. They must be mad at me.	Maybe they were just distracted or having a bad day. It's not necessarily about me.
Fortune Telling Predicting the future negatively without any real proof.	If I go to that event, I'll just be ignored, and it'll be awful.	I don't know for sure what will happen. Maybe I'll meet someone interesting or have a good time.
All-or-Nothing Thinking Seeing things in extremes: either you're a total success or a complete failure.	If I don't say something perfect, people will think I'm stupid.	No one expects perfection. Even if I stumble, people will still see my good qualities.
Mental Filtering Focusing only on the negative and ignoring the positive.	I embarrassed myself once in that conversation, so it was a total disaster.	Sure, I made one mistake, but the rest of the conversation went fine!
Doesn't Count Dismissing positive experiences or compliments as insignificant or flukes.	Yeah, they invited me, but they were just being polite. It doesn't count.	If they didn't want me there, they wouldn't have invited me. I do matter.
Personalization Blaming yourself for things outside your control.	They seemed upset. It must be something I did.	Their mood may have nothing to do with me.
"Should" Statements Placing unrealistic expectations on yourself.	I should always have everything together.	I'm doing my best, and that's enough.

> Thinking errors are the mind's way of keeping us isolated.
> Catching them is the first step to breaking free.

How to Start Changing These Thought Patterns
Catch the thought.
- When a negative thought appears, pause.
- Ask yourself: What am I telling myself right now?

Question if it's true.
- Is this a fact or an assumption?
- Would I say this to a friend?

Reframe it.
- Swap the self-judgment for self-compassion.
- Find a balanced, supportive way to see the situation.

Here's a tip: if you catch yourself thinking *What if...* this may be a red flag that you are **catastrophizing** (thinking about the worst thing that can happen).

Also, words like *always, never, and nothing* may be a warning sign for **overgeneralization** (making conclusions based on one or a few bad experiences).

Your brain is rewiring, give it time. When you first start trying to reframe those negative thoughts, it can feel a bit awkward. This is normal! Our brains get used to certain thought patterns, and shifting them takes time. But here's the good news: the more you practice it, the easier it gets. Eventually, you'll find that self-kindness starts to take the place of that nagging self-criticism. And when that shift happens? It really changes everything!

It's time to stop being so hard on yourself. The way you talk to yourself really matters! It influences everything in your life. How you carry yourself in conversations, deal with challenges, take risks, and even how others treat you are all shaped by your self-talk. Being tough on yourself is not the way to take responsibility for your failures and push yourself to improve. In fact, research reveals that not only is the opposite true, but that those who embrace self-compassion tend to be more motivated, more resilient, and significantly less likely to throw in the towel after a setback. It turns out that kindness to ourselves could be the key to unlocking our true potential.

It's easy to believe that being hard on yourself is what keeps you growing, but the truth is, self-criticism shrinks your world. You don't need to be perfect to be worthy of connection. You just need to be human. When you learn to meet yourself with the kindness you'd offer a friend, everything begins to shift.

What This Means: The way you speak to yourself matters. Harsh self-talk doesn't make you stronger; it makes you smaller. Replacing criticism with compassion doesn't mean letting yourself off the hook; it means holding yourself with care while still aiming to grow.

Why It Matters: Self-compassion builds resilience. When you're kinder to yourself, you're more willing to take risks, try again, and show up fully. It's not softness. It's strength. And it's a critical part of building the internal safety that leads to real social confidence.

What Comes Next: Catch your inner critic in action. When you notice a self-critical thought, pause and ask, *would I say this to someone I care about?* Then practice saying something kinder, even if it feels awkward at first. That's not weakness. It's emotional strength in motion.

> *"Change the way you look at things,*
> *and the things you look at change."*
>
> – Dr. Wayne Dyer

Chapter 7

Social Anxiety: A Way Out

*"Courage doesn't mean you don't get afraid.
Courage means you don't let fear stop you."*
— Bethany Hamilton

In 2023, the National Institute of Mental Health reported that about 15 million adults in the U.S., or 7.1% of the population, live with something called social anxiety disorder. That's not just feeling a little nervous before a meeting or overthinking what you said at a party (though we've all been there). Social anxiety disorder means that social situations almost always trigger fear. It sticks around, and it messes with the important stuff like relationships, career, school, life.

Here's what most people don't realize: this doesn't just show up out of nowhere in adulthood. The average age of onset is 13, and it often starts as early as 8 years old.

Let that sink in.

Right when kids are trying to figure out who they are, how to make friends, how to fit in, and where they belong, boom, that's when social anxiety creeps in. It's like trying to build confidence on a shaky bridge while everyone's watching. And if you've ever been the kid who got laughed at in front of the class or bullied for just being yourself, you know how fast one bad moment can burn into your memory.

Social anxiety doesn't just affect people with an official diagnosis. You might not have a therapist's note or a checklist that says, "Yep, you've got it." And yet... maybe you still panic a little before group conversations. Maybe your heart pounds when you speak up in a meeting. Maybe you avoid certain situations altogether just to dodge the fear.

That counts. That matters.

Let's be clear: social anxiety isn't just shyness. It's not being "a little introverted." It's your mind rewriting harmless moments into disaster. It's overanalyzing every sentence after you've said it. It's walking into a room and immediately wondering if everyone's already judged you. It's exhausting. And you're not weak. You're stuck in a loop your brain created to protect you from pain..

Feeling anxious in social situations is part of being human. We're wired for connection. We care what people think, and that's not a flaw. But when that caring turns into chronic fear, when it controls your decisions or shrinks your life down to something smaller than what you want, that's where we draw the line.

This chapter isn't about diagnosing you. It's about acknowledging your experience. Whether you meet the criteria for social anxiety disorder or simply feel small in big social spaces, this chapter offers insight, tools, and a path forward.

Not to "fix" you, because you're not broken, but to offer insight, tools, and a path forward.

Social Anxiety and Fear of Rejection

We're naturally built to connect with others, which makes us look for friendships and social interactions. At the same time, we've got this instinct to spot threats and steer clear of danger. Our brains view being alone as a threat, so really, what we're dealing with here is a fear of rejection. It's like this tug-of-war we deal with. On one hand, we really want to build connections, but on the other, we're hesitant to let our guards down.

If you happen to struggle with social anxiety, don't be too hard on yourself. It's really not your fault. Back in the day, getting rejected by your group was a serious issue. Imagine living thousands of years ago when being kicked out of your tribe could literally be a matter of life or death! So, it makes sense that even today, the fear of rejection feels so intense. Our brains still see it as a big deal, as if casual conversations or first dates are potentially life-threatening situations.

Here's what's happening behind the scenes. When you feel social anxiety, your brain's **amygdala** (the fear center) goes into overdrive. It sends signals that trigger your fight-or-flight response: your heart races, your breathing changes, and your mind starts scanning for "danger" (even though there isn't any).

Many people end up avoiding social situations just to escape the intense fear of being judged, embarrassed, or rejected. It seems like a good idea at first. Who wouldn't want relief from that fear? But here's the catch: every time you dodge those situations, it actually makes the anxiety worse. That's because your brain starts linking socializing with danger.

This is a tough cycle to break!

Social anxiety feels so real because your brain cherry-picks moments of discomfort and uses them as evidence that you're socially inadequate. But just because your brain tells you something, it doesn't mean it's true. This is exactly what happened to Charlie.

Charlie's Story

Charlie is a 30-year-old teacher who desperately wanted to date but couldn't get past his fear of rejection. He'd swipe through dating apps but never send a message. If he managed to get to a date, his mind raced with self-doubt:

- *What if I run out of things to say?*
- *What if they secretly think I'm boring?*
- *What if I embarrass myself and they laugh about me later?*

Every time he had an awkward conversation, he saw it as proof that he was bad at dating. So he avoided it. He threw himself into work, telling himself, *I'm too busy to date right now*—but deep down, he knew the real reason. The fear of rejection kept him stuck. But what Charlie didn't realize yet was this: **His fear wasn't about dating itself. It was about how he talked to himself.**

Charlie knew he wanted to date, but every time he thought about putting himself out there, a voice in his head (his inner critic) shut him down.

- *You're going to embarrass yourself.*

- *You're not interesting enough to keep a conversation going.*
- *Why would they pick you when they could date someone more confident?*

Sound familiar? Social anxiety isn't just about how others see you. It's about how you see yourself. And when that inner voice is constantly feeding you worst-case scenarios and self-doubt, it's no wonder social situations feel overwhelming. Your inner critic isn't telling the truth. It's telling you a fear-based story.

Charlie sat in his car after the date, replaying the night in his head like a scene from a movie. But instead of a highlight reel of what went well, his brain zeroed in on every moment that felt even slightly awkward.

- *She checked her phone once... Was she bored?*
- *There was a long pause after I made that joke... Maybe it wasn't funny.*
- *She hugged me goodbye but didn't say anything about seeing me again. That probably means she's not interested.*

By the time he got home, Charlie had convinced himself the date had been a disaster.

But was that actually true?

Or was his brain playing tricks on him?

Here's what was really happening:

Mind Reading: Charlie assumed he knew exactly what his date was thinking. She checked her phone, so she must be bored. But in reality, he had no idea. Maybe she was checking a work message or looking at the time.

Catastrophizing: Charlie took small moments and blew them out of proportion. *That one awkward pause ruined everything.* In reality, every conversation has pauses, and they don't mean disaster.

Personalization: Charlie believed everything that happened was about him. *She didn't mention a second date, so I must have done something wrong.* But what if she was nervous too? Or just someone who prefers to process things before making plans?

Social anxiety distorts reality like a warped mirror, making small things look bigger than they are. The problem wasn't that Charlie's date went badly, but how he interpreted it.

Charlie learns to challenge his thoughts.

Then, a week later, something unexpected happened: she texted him first. All those assumptions, all that overanalyzing… it had been completely wrong. That's when it hit Charlie: fear-based thoughts aren't facts. They were just guesses. Guesses are based on anxiety, not reality. Once he learned to spot these mental traps, he began catching his thoughts in real time.

- *Wait, am I mind-reading right now?*
- *Am I assuming one small moment defines the entire interaction?*
- *Is there another possible explanation that isn't about me?*

The more he did this, the more he realized that his social anxiety had been lying to him all along.

How to Handle Your Inner Critic

The next time your inner critic tries to hijack your brain, use these steps:

Step 1: Catch the Thought

What's the story my brain is telling me right now?

Step 2: Identify the Distortion

Am I mind reading someone's thoughts?

Am I catastrophizing one moment?

Am I personalizing something that might not be about me?

Step 3: Flip the Script

Ask yourself: *What's another possible explanation?*

Instead of: *They must think I'm awkward.*

Try: *Maybe they're just tired or distracted.*

Instead of: *I ruined that conversation.*

Try: *Every conversation has pauses. It doesn't mean failure.*

Bottom line: Your thoughts are not facts.

Charlie's biggest breakthrough wasn't learning how to date. It was learning how to challenge his thoughts. When he stopped believing every anxious thought, his anxiety lost power over him.

The same can be true for you. Social anxiety doesn't mean you're bad at socializing. It just means your brain is working overtime to keep you "safe." But safety isn't the goal here. Connection is.

When You Feel Awkward

Charlie had been on a handful of dates now, but there was one thing he still hadn't mastered: **awkward moments**.

Despite everything he had learned about challenging his inner critic, he still found himself overanalyzing every silence, every pause in conversation.

Whenever there was a quiet moment, he panicked, thinking, *I have to fill this space* or *she'll think I'm boring*. If he stumbled over his words, his mind immediately jumped to, *she probably thinks I'm weird*. Sound familiar?

The truth is, awkwardness isn't about what happens. It's about how we interpret it. But the truth is, those *cringeworthy* moments? Most people barely notice.

People Aren't Noticing as Much as You Think

Have you ever left a conversation obsessing over something dumb you think you said, only to realize later that no one else even remembers it? That's because of the **spotlight effect**—our brain's tendency to believe people are paying way more attention to us than they actually are. The truth is, most people are too wrapped up in their own thoughts to analyze every word you say. The tiny moment you keep replaying in your head? They probably forgot about it within five minutes.

Charlie learned about the spotlight effect and can now use this to his advantage. On one of his dates, Charlie tripped over his words while telling a story. Normally, he would have spiraled. *Ugh, I sound so awkward!* But instead, he reminded himself: *she's probably not analyzing this as much as I am*. And guess what? She didn't even react—she just laughed and kept the conversation going because it wasn't a big deal.

What Actually Makes Conversations Awkward?

Most awkward moments don't really come from the situation itself, but rather from how we react to it. It's funny how conversations can feel uncomfortable when we start panicking or over-apologizing. When you say, "Sorry, I'm so awkward," it can make the other person feel like they have to reassure you, which only adds to the awkwardness. Also, avoiding eye contact, fidgeting, or crossing your arms can make it seem like you're not interested or don't want to be there.

When it comes to appearing more confident, small adjustments can make a world of difference. Picture this: you're in a conversation and slip up on your words. Instead of panicking or dwelling on it, why not own the moment? Laugh it off and keep the vibe light. This not only helps you seem more at ease but also makes you far more likable to those around you.

And let's talk body language. Good eye contact, paired with a relaxed posture, such as leaning in slightly, can do wonders. It shows that you're genuinely interested in the other person and excited to engage. So next time you find yourself in a conversation, remember these simple tips. Embrace the moment, stay relaxed, and watch your confidence shine!

How to Recover From an Awkward Moment

Step 1: Breathe

Instead of panicking, take a slow breath. Awkwardness often feels worse internally than it looks externally.

Step 2: Normalize It

Instead of over-apologizing, make light of it.

- "Oops, I blanked for a sec... thanks for your patience."
- "Wow, that was a weird pause. Let's just pretend it didn't happen."
- "That sentence did not come out the way I intended. Ignore me!"
- "Wow, that was an awkward silence. Let's pretend it never happened."

This shows that you don't take yourself too seriously, which instantly makes other people feel more comfortable too.

Step 3: Redirect the Focus

Instead of spiraling about what just happened, shift the conversation back to the other person.

- "Tell me more about that trip you took!"
- "I need to hear the rest of that story you were telling me."
- "Wait, I just realized I never asked how your week's been!"

When you redirect the conversation, the moment passes more quickly than you think.

For the first time, Charlie didn't spiral. He didn't try to fix it. He just laughed it off, and to his surprise, so did she.

On one of his dates, Charlie experienced the worst-case scenario. He made a joke, his date didn't laugh, and there was a long silence. In the past, this would have sent him into full panic mode. He would have mumbled an apology, stared at the table, or convinced himself he ruined the whole night.

But instead, he did something different. He smiled, shrugged, and said, "Okay, so that one didn't land. I'll try again later." His date laughed immediately. Not at him, but with him. The awkwardness was gone. And in that moment, Charlie realized awkwardness isn't about avoiding mistakes. It's about handling them with confidence.

The next time you feel yourself overthinking an awkward moment, remind yourself:

The moment passes faster than you think.

People don't remember small slip-ups.
Confidence isn't about perfection.
It's about rolling with it.

Rejection: It's Not as Personal as You Think

Charlie had come a long way. He was finally putting himself out there, challenging his inner critic, managing awkwardness with humor, and staying present in conversations.

But there was still one thing that terrified him: rejection. It wasn't just about dating. He felt the same fear in work meetings, group outings, and even casual social settings.

Any time he sensed even the slightest disinterest from someone, his brain went into overdrive:

- *They don't actually like me.*
- *I must have done something wrong.*
- *I should just stop trying.*

So when a date he really liked didn't text him back, it sent him into a spiral. But here's what Charlie hadn't yet realized: Rejection is almost never as personal as it feels.

Rejection feels so big because it activates the same part of the brain as physical pain. That's why it hurts. Your brain processes social exclusion like an injury. But the real problem isn't rejection itself. It's the story we tell ourselves about rejection.

Charlie's old way of thinking:

She didn't text me back. That means I said something wrong, and she wasn't interested.

What was actually true?

Maybe she was busy. Maybe she had personal stuff going on. Maybe she was seeing someone else. None of those things had anything to do with Charlie's worth.

Rejection doesn't define you. It's just data. What if, instead of seeing rejection as proof of failure, you saw it as a filter that leads you to the right people? For example:

Instead of: *They weren't interested, so I must not be good enough.*

Try: *Not everyone is going to click, and that's okay. I'm looking for the ones who do.*

Charlie learns to stop taking rejection personally.

One night, after yet another date left him ghosted, Charlie found himself at a crossroads. He had two options to choose from.

Option 1: Dive headfirst into a spiral of self-doubt, dissecting every moment and word from the date until he convinced himself he was unworthy of love.

Option 2: Hit the pause button and take a fresh perspective. This time, he chose Option 2, reminding himself, *This isn't a reflection of me. People's actions are about their own priorities, feelings, and situations.*

He offered himself another powerful reframe: *Someone else's lack of interest doesn't diminish my value.* With a newfound clarity, he thought, *if it's not meant to be, I'd rather know now and keep moving forward.* And that's when it hit him: Rejection isn't about proving your worth. It's about finding the right fit.

How to Handle Rejection

Step 1: Normalize It

Everyone experiences rejection. Even the most confident, attractive, charismatic people. Rejection isn't an attack. It's a normal part of life.

Step 2: Separate Feelings from Facts

It's okay to feel disappointed, but that feeling doesn't mean you did anything wrong. Check the story you're telling yourself.

Instead of: *They ghosted me, so I must have been boring.*

Try: *I have no idea why they didn't text back. It could be a hundred different things, and none of them are about me.*

Step 3: Flip the Script

What if you were the one who wasn't interested? Would it mean the other person wasn't good enough? Of course not. It would just mean you weren't a fit.

So why assume that when the roles are reversed?

Step 4: Move Forward (Don't Let It Close You Off)

Instead of seeing rejection as proof you should stop trying, see it as redirection toward something better. Rejection doesn't mean you're not good enough. It just means this wasn't the right fit.

Charlie's Breakthrough: Moving On Instead of Looking Back

A few months after his last rejection spiral, Charlie had another date that fizzled out. But this time, instead of obsessing, he shrugged it off. Not because he didn't care. Not because he didn't want things to work out. But because he finally understood that rejection isn't a verdict on his worth, it's just part of the process.

And the best part? The moment he stopped overanalyzing, he started enjoying dating a lot more. No more pressure. No more feeling like every interaction was a test. Just a real connection with the people who actually matched him.

Bottom line: You're not for everyone, and that's a good thing. The next time rejection stings, remind yourself:

- The right people won't need convincing.
- If it's not a fit, it's not failure, it's redirection.
- Rejection doesn't define your worth. It just helps you find the right people faster.

Charlie's journey with social anxiety wasn't about waking up one day suddenly fearless. Instead, he learned something even more powerful:

Fear doesn't have to disappear for you to move forward.

He still had moments of self-doubt. But now, he had tools, ways to manage those feelings so they no longer controlled his choices.

Along the way, Charlie learned something important: People aren't watching you as closely as you might think. He also discovered that feeling awkward isn't a big deal. It's just a passing moment. Plus, he realized that rejection doesn't mean you're not good enough; it's really just a chance to find a new path. Most importantly, Charlie figured out that the best way to tackle social anxiety is to stop waiting around and start taking action. Keep moving forward, you've got this!

Tools for Managing Social Anxiety in the Moment

So, you've mastered the art of challenging that pesky inner critic, navigated through those awkward moments, and reframed rejection into a stepping stone for growth. But there's still one hurdle to leap over. What happens when social anxiety crashes the party? Don't worry, because I'm going to share with you five of my favorite tools. The key is to practice ahead of time. By rehearsing your strategies ahead of time, you will boost your confidence and turn those anxious situations into opportunities for connection and fun.

1. The 5-4-3-2-1 Grounding Technique

Anxiety lives in the future. What if I mess up? What if they don't like me? So the best way to shut it down is to **anchor yourself in the present**. Use this quick grounding exercise anytime you feel anxiety creeping in:

5 things you can see (the window, your hands, a light fixture).
4 things you can touch (the table, your clothing, your phone).
3 things you can hear (background chatter, footsteps, music).
2 things you can smell (coffee, perfume, fresh air).
1 thing you can taste (gum, water, whatever you last ate).

By the time you reach one, your brain has shifted out of anxiety mode and into the present.

2. The 5-Second Rule

Beat Anxiety Before It Talks You Out of It

One of the biggest mistakes people with social anxiety make is **overthinking before speaking or taking action**. By the time you build up the nerve to say something, the moment has already passed. It can be so easy to talk yourself out of starting a conversation before it even starts.

- *What if I say the wrong thing?*
- *What if they don't want to talk to me?*
- *What if I embarrass myself?*

Has this ever happened to you? It's definitely happened to me. And that's when I discovered Mel Robbins' 5-Second Rule.

> **The Rule:** If you feel the urge to do something but hesitate, count **5-4-3-2-1 GO.**

This works because social anxiety thrives on hesitation. The longer you wait, the more reasons your brain finds to talk you out of it.

- *I should introduce myself...* but what if they think I'm weird?
- *I want to say hi...* but I don't want to interrupt.
- *I should send that text...* but maybe they won't respond.

The usual pattern?

Wait too long → feel awkward → miss the chance.

Next time, try something different.

Count: **5... 4... 3... 2... 1... GO.**

And before your brain can argue, walk over and say something simple. The conversation started. And just like that, the hardest part is over.

Want to start a conversation?

5-4-3-2-1 → Then say something.

Feeling the urge to leave early out of discomfort?

5-4-3-2-1 → Stay five more minutes.

Nervous to send a text or invitation?

5-4-3-2-1 → hit send.

The more you take action, the more confident you'll feel. And remember: It's not about saying the perfect thing. It's about saying something.

Bottom line: The longer you hesitate, the harder it feels. The next time social anxiety makes you freeze, don't wait, count down from five, and move. The moment you take action, you prove to your brain *I can do this, and I don't have to be perfect—I just have to show up.*

3. The "Worst-Case Scenario" Reframe

Charlie's biggest fear on dates was saying something awkward. But then he learned a simple trick that changed everything: Whenever he felt anxious, he asked himself, "What's the worst that could happen?" For example:

Fear: *What if I say something weird?*
Worst-case scenario: *They might think I'm a little awkward.*
Reality check: *Would that be devastating? No. Would I survive? Yes.*

The next time social anxiety flares up, pause and play it out:
- What's the absolute worst thing that could happen?
- Would I still be okay afterward?
- Has something like this happened before, and did it turn out fine?

99% of the time, the worst-case scenario is nowhere near as bad as your anxiety makes it seem.

4. The "Turn the Spotlight Around" Trick

Social anxiety makes you hyper-aware of yourself, how you sound, how you look, and what others think of you. But here's the thing:

> *Most people are too busy thinking about*
> *themselves to be analyzing you.*

Charlie used to think, *everyone is paying attention to me.* But once he realized everyone else was worrying about themselves, he relaxed.

> **Trick:** When you feel self-conscious, shift the focus outward.

Instead of thinking: *Do they like me?*
Think: *Do I like them?*

Instead of worrying: *Am I being interesting?*
Try: Get curious about them.

Instead of obsessing: *What do they think of me?*
Notice something about them and ask a question.

When you make genuine curiosity your goal, conversations feel more natural, and anxiety takes a back seat.

5. The "One Conversation at a Time" Rule

Social anxiety makes big social situations feel overwhelming. Walking into a party, a wedding, or a networking event? Charlie used to think, *I have to be "on" all night.* That's exhausting.

Then, he flipped his approach.

Instead of trying to "perform" in a room full of people, he focused on one person at a time.

Instead of: *I have to impress everyone.*
   Think: *I just need to have one good conversation.*

Instead of: *I have to be entertaining all night.*
   Think: *I can just listen, be present, and connect.*

Focusing on one small interaction at a time takes the pressure off and makes socializing way less intimidating.

Social anxiety isn't something you think your way out of. It's something you take action against. Next time you feel anxiety creeping in, try one of these tools:
- ✔ 5-4-3-2-1 Grounding (to get out of your head)
- ✔ The 3-Second Rule (so you don't overthink)
- ✔ The Worst-Case Scenario Reframe (to calm fear)
- ✔ Turn the Spotlight Around
   (so you stop feeling on display)
- ✔ One Conversation at a Time
   (so you don't get overwhelmed)

And remember: Courage isn't the absence of anxiety. It's showing up anyway.

Social anxiety can make even everyday interactions feel like uphill climbs. But anxiety isn't a sign that something is wrong with you. It's a sign that says, "I want to connect, but I'm afraid." The way out isn't by forcing yourself to "just get over it." It's by learning to meet your fear with understanding, not judgment.

What This Means: Social anxiety is not your identity. It's a response. It doesn't mean you're broken. It means your nervous system is trying to protect you. But protection can sometimes go too far, holding you back from the very things that would help you feel safe.

Why It Matters: Understanding anxiety helps to soften its grip. When you stop seeing it as a flaw and start seeing it as a pattern, you gain power. You can begin choosing small moments of courage. Ones that stretch you without overwhelming you. That's how real change begins.

What Comes Next: Choose one low-stakes social moment this week to practice presence: a brief hello, eye contact, or staying in a conversation a few seconds longer. Progress doesn't have to be loud. It just has to be honest. Each small win is a step forward.

"You wouldn't worry so much about what others think of you if you realized how seldom they do."

– Eleanor Roosevelt

Chapter 8

You're More Likable Than You Think

"We suffer more in imagination than in reality."
— Seneca

Have you ever walked away from a conversation convinced you said the wrong thing? Maybe you worried that you talked too much, looked awkward, or didn't make the impression you wanted. Even if the other person laughed, nodded, or seemed engaged, you still found yourself overanalyzing every detail.

- Did I make sense?
- Were they just being polite?
- What if I sounded weird and they don't actually like me?

These doubts aren't just fleeting thoughts. They're part of a larger pattern of false beliefs that distort how we see ourselves socially. We hesitate before reaching out because we assume we'll be a burden. We hold back in conversations because we don't think people are that interested in what we have to say. We replay awkward moments over and over again, convinced they matter far more than they actually do.

And yet, none of these assumptions are actually true.

What if You're More Likable Than You Think?

For decades, social psychologists have studied how we perceive ourselves in social situations, and what they've discovered is eye-opening.

We assume people don't like us as much as we like them, but in reality, they often like us more than we think. We worry we're bothering people when we reach out, but research shows people appreciate it more than we expect. We hesitate to give compliments, fearing it will feel forced, but studies show that compliments actually mean more to people than we realize. We think people are scrutinizing our every awkward moment when, in reality, they're barely noticing.

The biggest irony? The fears that make us shrink back are usually completely unfounded. In this chapter, we'll break down the most common myths that make socializing feel harder than it is and reveal what psychology says is actually true. By the time you finish, you'll start seeing your interactions differently. With more confidence, more trust, and less self-doubt. Let's start with one of the biggest myths of all.

> We all crave connection, yet invisible myths about our worth and likability hold us back. These false beliefs keep us stuck in self-doubt. The moment we recognize them for what they are, we gain the freedom to connect authentically and with confidence.

The Liking Gap
You're More Liked Than You Think

Joe didn't want to come.

His sister, Marina, had been after him all week: "You're in town, you work remotely, and you can't stay inside playing Elden Ring forever. Come meet some actual humans." So here he was hovering near a cookie table in an elementary school gym, trying to look normal while fiddling with a paper plate of brownies and cheese cubes.

Eventually, someone—Marina's neighbor's friend, apparently—struck up a conversation with him near the drink table. Joe relaxed a little. They talked about indie game development, then movies, then work-from-home weirdness. It flowed easily. They even laughed a couple of times.

After a few minutes, the guy said, "It was really cool meeting you. Hope we run into each other again," and wandered off toward the raffle table.

Joe stood there, blinking. *Was that okay? Did I ramble too much? Maybe I came on too strong. Maybe he was just being polite. I bet he's already forgotten half of what I said.*

The Liking Gap: What It Is

Joe's thoughts are familiar and surprisingly universal.

Have you ever had a great conversation with someone, only to later convince yourself they were just being nice? You replay every detail like a post-game analysis:
- *Did I talk too much?*
- *Was I interesting enough?*

- *What if they didn't actually like me at all?*

Meanwhile, the other person is walking away thinking: *That was such a great conversation. I really enjoyed that.*

> This disconnect is called **the liking gap**, and it's one of the most persistent illusions in social life.

Why the Liking Gap Happens

We experience our conversations through a **lens of self-judgment**. We zoom in on every awkward pause, every word we fumbled, every moment we weren't perfectly polished. It feels like everyone else must have noticed.

But they didn't.

The other person isn't replaying your exact words. They're walking away with a simple impression: *Did I enjoy being around them?* And if the answer is yes, your awkward word choices and nervous jokes don't matter.

Ironically, the more you care about how you come across, the more likely it is that others actually liked the conversation. Why? Because people are drawn to those who are present, engaged, and emotionally tuned in. Your overthinking is often a sign that you were paying attention and that's exactly what makes people feel seen.

Back to Joe...

Joe wandered off toward the hallway, already editing everything he said in his head. *I should've asked more questions.*

That story about the design glitch probably went on too long. He probably thinks I'm weird.

Across the gym, the guy was now talking to Marina. "Your brother's great," he said. "Super interesting guy. I had no idea indie game development was that involved. We had a really good chat."

Marina smiled. "I'll let him know. He's convinced he tanked it."

The guy raised an eyebrow. "Really? He seemed chill. I liked him."

And that's the liking gap in action: you think others like you less than they do, when in reality, they're probably thinking the opposite.

How to Work With the Liking Gap

You may never fully silence the post-social spiral. But you can learn to second-guess your self-doubt instead of yourself.

Reality Check #1: Flip the roles.

Ask yourself: *If someone else had said what I just said, would I be judging them?* Probably not. You'd be thinking, they were nice, or they were real.

Reality Check #2: Look for real signs.

Did they laugh? Stay engaged? Smile? Say something affirming? That's data. Use it.

Reality Check #3: Assume likability, not awkwardness.

Try flipping your default belief. Instead of *I probably came off weird,* tell yourself: *They probably liked me more than I realize.*

Bottom Line

The liking gap isn't a personal flaw. It's a thinking habit, a trick of the mind. But once you see it, you don't have to believe it anymore.

You're more liked than you think.

You're probably doing better than you realize.

And the people you meet? Most of them are just glad you talked to them at all.

Under-Sociality
You're Not a Burden

Joe had nearly talked himself out of coming.

The whole ride to the event, he'd rehearsed excuses to leave early: a fake work call, a "forgotten" deadline, anything to avoid lingering in a room full of strangers making small talk over lukewarm decaf and homemade brownies.

But what almost kept him from speaking at all was something quieter and harder to catch.

As he stood by the drink table earlier that evening, he noticed a guy around his age scanning the room. It would've been so easy to say something. Anything. Comment on the coffee, joke about the snack selection, or mention the chaotic energy of folding chairs and raffle tables.

But Joe didn't move.

He probably doesn't want to be bothered.

He already looks like he's waiting for someone.

I'll just come off awkward. Or worse, needy.

That inner monologue, the one that talks us out of reaching out? That has a name. Psychologists call it **under-sociality**, and it keeps us disconnected more than we realize.

Under-Sociality: What It Is

Under-sociality is the false belief that **others don't want to hear from us, include us, or connect with us.**

It's the story we tell ourselves in quiet moments:
- *They're too busy.*
- *If they wanted to talk, they'd come to me.*
- *They don't really care what I have to say.*

It makes us hesitate before texting a friend, joining a group chat, or speaking up in a meeting. It convinces us that our presence might be more of an interruption than a contribution.

But here's the twist: **the science says we're wrong.**

Why Under-Sociality Happens

We're not antisocial. We're cautious.

We've been taught to value independence, not neediness. And somewhere along the way, many of us internalized the idea that initiating connection is risky or imposing. That we'll be seen as clingy, or awkward, or trying too hard.

But research shows the opposite is true. In dozens of studies, people who reached out—whether to make small talk, reconnect with a friend, or simply say hi—**consistently underestimated how appreciated and welcomed their outreach would be.**

In short, you think you're bothering people... but people are actually waiting for someone like you to make the first move.

Back to Joe...

Joe had nearly walked away from the drink table when he heard the other guy laugh softly at something on his phone. That tiny moment gave Joe the courage to say something.

"You drink coffee this late? Bold move."

It wasn't brilliant. It wasn't even especially funny. But it was enough.

The conversation that followed wasn't perfect, but it was human. And in the end, the guy had circled back to say he genuinely enjoyed talking to Joe. That connection never would've happened if Joe had listened to his inner hesitation.

How to Work With Under-Sociality

The biggest lie under-sociality tells you is this: *You're the only one who feels this way.*

You're not. And here's how to push through the hesitation next time:

Reality Check #1: Assume warmth, not indifference.

Most people enjoy being talked to more than they let on. Try this thought: *They'd probably like someone to talk to, too.*

Reality Check #2: The "I don't want to bother them" fear is mutual.

The reason people don't reach out to you? They're thinking the exact same thing.

Reality Check #3: You're not imposing, you're including.

Initiating is a gift. It makes people feel noticed, welcomed, and valued. You're not crashing something, and you're inviting someone into something real.

Bottom Line

What if, instead of assuming we're bothering people, we assumed they'd be happy to hear from us?

Try it. You might be surprised.

The next time you hesitate to send a text, join a conversation, or speak up in a group, remind yourself:

You are not a burden.

People are waiting for you to take the first step.

You matter more than you think.

The Spotlight Effect
People Aren't Watching You That Closely

Charlie stood behind the raffle table, sipping lukewarm coffee from a thin paper cup and wondering why he always felt so awkward at these events.

He liked people. He was a good teacher. He knew most of the parents here and had probably spoken to their kids that very week. But something about standing off-duty in a brightly lit gym—plastic raffle prizes behind him and PTA conversations swirling around—made him feel... exposed.

Earlier, Marina had passed by with a friendly smile. For a split second, Charlie forgot her name. He covered it with a quick "Hey there!" and hoped his tone sounded casual enough to pass for familiarity. But now, standing here replaying that moment, his thoughts spun:

She probably thinks I'm rude.

Or dismissive. Or completely disinterested.

Did I sound fake? Did she notice the hesitation? Why do I always mess these things up when I want to come across well?

He looked down at his coffee, willing himself to blend into the tablecloth.

The Spotlight Effect: What It Is

The *spotlight effect* is the illusion that **people are paying more attention to us than they really are**, especially to our perceived mistakes or awkward moments.

You trip, stumble, forget a name, say something clunky. And suddenly it feels like a bright light has turned on above your head. Everyone must've seen it. Everyone must be judging it. But they aren't. The reality is, most people didn't notice. And the few who did? They've already forgotten.

Why the Spotlight Effect Happens

We live in our own heads. Everything we say, feel, or do feels magnified because we're experiencing it firsthand. It's like watching your life through a high-def close-up camera while everyone else is catching a quick, fuzzy glimpse from across the room.

We assume our slip-ups matter to others as much as they matter to us. But they don't. Why? Because everyone else is doing the same thing, anxiously monitoring themselves, not you. Even if someone notices a moment of awkwardness, it rarely sticks. People don't remember our small stumbles, they remember how we made them feel overall. And one imperfect moment doesn't define that.

Back to Charlie…

Fifteen minutes after the name slip, Marina returned to the raffle table. She smiled again.

"Hey Charlie, did you see who won the cookie tower? I'm hoping it wasn't me, I'll eat the whole thing."

Charlie blinked. "No idea. But I hope it was you. I'm rooting for the chaos."

They laughed. And just like that, the air cleared. No weird tension. No judgment. Just two people sharing a light moment.

Charlie realized something in that second: *The thing I was obsessing over? She probably never even noticed.*

And even if she had, it clearly didn't matter.

How to Work With the Spotlight

You might always get a little self-conscious in social situations. That's okay. The trick is remembering that your inner critic doesn't have access to other people's heads.

Reality Check #1: Flip the situation.

If someone forgot your name, would you dwell on it?

Would you think they were rude or broken?

No. You'd probably shrug it off.

Reality Check #2: Everyone else is thinking about themselves.

They're not watching you. They're wondering how they look, sound, or come across.

Reality Check #3: Awkward moments evaporate.

That cringeworthy thing you did? Forgotten.

That stumble or fumble? Gone.

Unless you draw a spotlight to it, most people move on immediately.

Bottom Line

You're not being watched.

You're not being analyzed.

You're just another person in the room, and that's a good thing. So the next time you start replaying a tiny misstep like it was a headline moment, remind yourself: **You're not onstage. You're not under review. You're just human.**

And everyone else is too distracted by their own self-consciousness to notice yours.

Social Comparison and The Digital Mirror When Life Feels Like a Performance

Marina stood near the cookie table, trying to look busy by rearranging napkins and nibbling the corner of a brownie. Conversations buzzed around her: parents laughing, someone calling out raffle numbers, a playlist of upbeat acoustic covers humming over the speakers.

She smiled when people made eye contact, nodded along when someone passed by, and said, "Glad you could make it," but underneath it all, she felt like a placeholder in a scene already underway.

Earlier that day, she'd seen an Instagram post from three parents who were also here tonight. They'd shared a photo in front of the school gym: coordinated outfits, matching water bottles, one kid holding a hand-lettered "Fall Festival!" sign. The caption was witty. The lighting was flawless. Marina, in contrast, had changed outfits three times and still felt like she'd shown up as the before photo in someone else's transformation reel.

They already belong, her brain whispered. You're just visiting.

Social Comparison: What It Is

Social comparison is our brain's way of gauging where we stand in the world: who's doing better, who's more liked, who's more together.

But here's the problem: we're comparing ourselves to an illusion. In social situations, especially ones like this, comparison sneaks in fast:

- *They seem more confident.*
- *She already knows everyone.*
- *Why don't I have a friend group like that?*

And when social media joins the mix, the distortion magnifies.

The Digital Mirror: Why Comparison Now Feels Like Performance

It's not just that we compare. We **perform** too.

Social media has created a digital mirror that reflects back not who we are, but who we think we should be. We scroll through curated, edited, and often staged moments—polished families, clever party captions, smiling selfies in good light—and mistake those for reality.

So we filter. Pose. Polish. Post. Not to lie, but to keep up.

We imagine we're being seen all the time, even when we're not online. And that imagined gaze follows us into rooms like school gyms, work events, friend dinners. It whispers, *Do I look like I belong here?* It makes us feel like we have to earn our place in real time, with every word, every outfit, every smile.

But no one is really watching you that closely. They're too busy editing their own feed online or in their mind.

Back to Marina...

As she reached for another napkin she didn't need, a woman from her son's soccer team appeared beside her.

"I'm really glad you came tonight," the woman said, eyes kind. "I've been standing here for ten minutes trying to work up the courage to say hi to you."

Marina blinked. "Wait... me?"

The woman laughed. "Yeah! You seem so confident. Like you already know everyone."

Marina stared for a second, then actually laughed. "That's... hilarious. I've been feeling like the outsider all night."

"Same," the woman said. They both smiled.

For a moment, the imaginary scoreboard faded. They were just two humans, awkward and kind, glad they spoke up.

How to Work With Social Comparison and Digital Performance Pressure

You can't stop your brain from scanning for comparisons. But you can remind yourself what's real and what's edited.

Reality Check #1: You're comparing your full self to someone else's highlight reel.

You see your mess. They're showing you their lighting.

It's not a fair fight.

Reality Check #2: No one's thinking about you as much as you think.

Everyone's trying to look like they belong.

Most people feel like outsiders in some way.

Reality Check #3: Life isn't a feed.

There are no likes here. No filters. No captions.

Just people, trying.

Bottom Line

Comparison doesn't reflect the truth. It reflects longing. And when you believe the lie that everyone else has it together, you miss the moments that are actually real, like a stranger turning into a friend over broken cookies and a kind word.

You are not behind.

You are not less than.

You are already enough, as you are.

The Compliment Gap
Say It Out Loud

Marina hadn't planned to say anything.

The woman standing next to her at the cookie table had just helped organize the entire school event. She'd wrangled volunteers, coordinated with teachers, managed allergy-friendly snacks, and somehow still looked put together under fluorescent gym lights.

Marina had noticed. She wanted to say something. But then the familiar hesitation crept in:

She probably already knows she did a good job.
What if it sounds forced?
What if she thinks I'm being fake?

So she stayed quiet.

The moment passed.

And just like that, a tiny opportunity for connection—an easy moment of warmth—vanished under the weight of self-conscious doubt.

The Compliment Gap: What it Is

The *compliment gap* is **the tendency to withhold kind words**, not because we don't think them, but because we convince ourselves they'll land awkwardly or come off wrong.

It shows up like this:

- You admire someone's outfit but say nothing.
- You appreciate how a coworker skillfully led a meeting, but you keep your thoughts to yourself.

- You want to tell a friend they made your day... but the moment slips by.

We often underestimate the power of compliments and overestimate the likelihood of awkwardness. However, the reality is different:

People love hearing what you see in them.

Even confident people. Even polished ones.

Especially the ones who look like they've got it all together.

Why the Compliment Gap Happens

Giving a compliment feels vulnerable. You're putting emotion into the air and hoping it lands gently.

But most of us default to self-protection. We fear:

- Sounding cheesy.
- Being misunderstood.
- Getting it "wrong."

So we keep our admiration private. We stay safe. But in doing so, we **miss the chance to give someone else what they might desperately need to hear.**

Here's the twist: research consistently shows that people enjoy receiving compliments more than we think. Far more.

They're not awkward. They're affirming.

They make people feel seen.

They build trust and connection, sometimes in an instant.

Back to Marina...

Ten minutes later, Marina ran into the same woman in the hallway. Her arms were full of raffle tickets and water bottles. Before she could overthink it again, Marina said:

"Hey, I just wanted to say, you've really done an amazing job tonight. This whole thing runs because of people like you. I know that kind of effort doesn't always get noticed."

The woman froze, for a second, and her whole face softened.

"Wow," she said. "Thank you. I was honestly feeling like I'd dropped ten balls tonight."

Marina smiled. "From out here, it looks pretty seamless."

The woman laughed. "That means more than you know."

Marina walked away lighter, surprised at how good it felt to say something out loud that had been sitting in her chest the whole night. It hadn't been awkward. It had been real.

How to Close the Compliment Gap

You don't need perfect timing or poetic words. You just need to speak what's already true.

Reality Check #1: People never "already know."

Even confident people need reassurance. Even accomplished people second-guess themselves.

Reality Check #2: Kindness rarely feels weird.

You might feel nervous. But the other person? They're usually grateful, touched, sometimes even surprised.

Reality Check #3: Words can change someone's day.

A compliment doesn't have to be profound. It just has to be honest.

Bottom Line

If you think something kind, say it.

Your words could be the reminder someone needed.

Your compliment might land in the middle of their self-doubt.

Your voice might become the memory they replay when they're feeling unsure.

Say the thing. Give the credit.

Make the moment a little softer, for them and for you.

The Reciprocity Blind Spot
Stop Waiting for the First Move

Joe assumed if people liked him, they'd show it.

That had been his default setting for as long as he could remember. If someone wanted to be friends, they'd make plans. If someone valued his ideas, they'd ask for them. If someone cared, they'd text first. But more often than not, they didn't.

And over time, Joe started interpreting silence as disinterest.

They didn't reach out—so I must not matter that much.

They didn't invite me—so I probably wasn't wanted.

They haven't checked in—so I guess they've moved on.

He wasn't bitter, just confused. He showed up for people. So why didn't they do the same? What Joe didn't realize is this: **they were waiting too.**

Waiting for a sign.

Waiting for a nudge. Waiting for permission.

And that mutual waiting? It builds walls no one intended.

The Reciprocity Blind Spot: What It Is

The *reciprocity blind spot* is the belief that if someone really values us, they'll be the one to reach out first. But here's what psychology tells us: most people don't reach out, not because they don't care, but because **they're afraid they'll be rejected, ignored, or seen as intrusive.**

They're thinking:

- *You're probably busy.*
- *You'd reach out if you wanted to talk.*
- *I don't want to make it weird.*

So both people wait. Both people want a connection. And nothing happens.

Why This Happens

It's rooted in something called the *reciprocity principle*: the idea that people tend to mirror the energy and behavior they receive. If you pull back, they pull back. If you hesitate, they hesitate. And if you initiate? You often give them permission to engage.

The result? The connection we crave stays just out of reach, not because it's not there, but because we're waiting for someone else to go first.

Back to Joe...

That night, after the school event, Joe pulled out his phone. He hovered over a text thread with a friend he hadn't seen in months. They used to hang out every week. Then work got busy. Life happened. Now, it had been radio silence.

Joe stared at his phone. He hasn't reached out in forever. What if he's moved on? What if I text and it's just... awkward?

Then, almost against his own instincts, he typed: "Hey man, miss catching up. Want to grab coffee sometime soon?"

The reply came less than two minutes later: "YES. I was literally just thinking about you. I almost texted yesterday."

And just like that, the waiting loop broke.

How to Stop Waiting and Start Connecting

Initiating isn't needy. It's brave.

And usually, it's welcomed more than you expect.

Reality Check #1: People want to be invited.

Most people are relieved when you make the first move.

Reality Check #2: Silence isn't rejection.

It's often fear. Or distraction. Or uncertainty. Not disinterest.

Reality Check #3: Going first builds a deeper connection.

You're not chasing.

You're choosing to create the connection you want.

Bottom Line

We all want to feel wanted. But someone has to go first. Let that someone be you.

Reach out. Send the text. Make the plan.

Because the people you're waiting on? They're probably waiting on you too.

Emotional Contagion
You Don't Have to Be Impressive

Marina used to think connection came from saying the right thing. She'd prep for social situations like a mental dress rehearsal: what stories to share, what jokes might land, which parts of her life were interesting enough to mention. Especially in new cities, new schools, and unfamiliar rooms, she felt the need to prove she belonged.

But tonight, something shifted. After giving that compliment at the cookie table, she hadn't tried to be clever. She hadn't tried to be impressive. She just said something kind, and the woman lit up. Not because Marina was particularly witty or insightful... but because she saw her.

That moment stayed with Marina all night. For once, she hadn't been performing. And somehow, she'd connected more deeply than when she was.

Emotional Contagion: What It Is

Emotional contagion is the psychological phenomenon where **your emotions subtly influence the emotions of people around you.** It happens in micro-moments: through tone of voice, facial expressions, body language, and energy.

You've felt this before:

- When someone's laughter made you laugh before you even knew why.
- When being around a calm person helped you breathe more easily.
- When a friend's anxiety made you start to feel tense too.

We absorb each other's emotional states constantly. And we're not drawn to people because they're the smartest or funniest; we're drawn to how they make us feel.

Why This Happens

In social situations, we often put pressure on ourselves to be interesting. To say the right thing. To sound accomplished, articulate, or cool. But the truth is: **people don't remember your words. They remember your warmth**. They remember if you made them feel seen. If you gave them space to speak. If your energy felt open and kind.

Back to Marina…

Later that evening, Marina stood near the exit with a cup of lukewarm cider and a tired smile. A dad she barely knew walked by with his daughter and paused.

"Hey, I meant to say, you've got a really calm energy," he said. "It's nice. This whole thing's a little chaotic, and talking to you felt… grounding."

Marina blinked. "Oh… thank you. That's really kind of you to say."

She hadn't said anything brilliant. She hadn't tried to.
But her presence had done something good.

And for the first time in a while, she believed it didn't take more to be enough. Maybe it actually took less.

How to Tune Into Emotional Influence

You don't need to impress. You just need to show up in a way that people can feel.

Reality Check #1: You're already influencing the room.

Even your silence, your tone, your posture, it all speaks.

What is it saying?

Reality Check #2: Emotions are more contagious than opinions.

You don't need to win people over with logic.

Let them feel safety, kindness, or openness instead.

Reality Check #3: Presence is a gift.

You don't have to entertain or educate.

You just have to be there, genuinely.

Bottom Line

The most memorable people aren't always the loudest or most polished. They're the ones who made you feel calm when you were anxious, hopeful when you were discouraged, seen when you felt invisible. So stop trying to be impressive.

Just be real. That's what people remember anyway.

You're More Likable Than You Think
A New Way to See Yourself

If you've ever walked away from a conversation replaying everything you said…

If you've ever held back a compliment you meant to say…

If you've ever stayed quiet, convinced you'd come off awkward or out of place…

You're not alone. And more importantly, you're not broken. You're just human.

And these quiet distortions you've lived with, these blind spots, are not flaws in your personality. They're patterns. Common, predictable ones. And they lose power the moment we name them.

RECAP: The Blind Spots That Distort How We See Ourselves Socially

- **The Liking Gap**

  You think others like you less than they do.

  But you're usually more appreciated than you realize.

- **Under-Sociality**

  You assume others don't want to connect.

  But most people are more open than they look.

- **The Spotlight Effect**

  You think everyone notices your awkward moments.

  But they're too busy noticing their own.

- **Social Comparison and The Digital Mirror**

  You compare your real life to someone else's curated one.

  But they're filtering too, and you're not behind.

- **The Compliment Gap**

  You hesitate to say kind things.

  But people need your words more than you think.

- **The Reciprocity Blind Spot**

  You wait for others to go first.

  But they're waiting too.

- **Emotional Contagion**
  You try to be impressive.
  But what really connects people is how you make them feel.

I wish I'd known about these blind spots years ago. So many opportunities for connection passed me by, not because I didn't care, but because I thought I had to earn my way in. Be more interesting. Sound smarter. Look cooler. I didn't realize that my presence was already enough.

The first time I read about things like the liking gap and the spotlight effect, I felt something loosen inside me. Like, Oh. It's not just me. That small shift changed everything. It gave me permission to be more open. To show up imperfectly. To stop performing and start connecting.

And that's what I want for you too.

What This Means: You are far more likable than you've been led to believe. The voice in your head that questions your worth, replays awkward moments, or tells you not to reach out—it's not the truth. It's a habit. People aren't judging you nearly as much as you think. Most of them are just hoping someone like you will talk to them first.

Why It Matters: When you stop believing these false stories about yourself, you open the door to real connection. You stop holding back. You start showing up. Not as a version of yourself you think others want, but as yourself. That kind of confidence doesn't just make you feel better. It changes how people respond to you. It invites more warmth, more trust, and more genuine moments into your life.

What Comes Next: Try something small this week: Say hello first. Give the compliment. Reach out instead of waiting. It doesn't have to be big or bold. Just honest. Because the truth is you don't need to be more impressive. You just need to believe, a little more often, that you're already worth knowing.

Good news: You're already likable.
Bad news: That means your awkward jokes
are just part of the charm.

Part 3

Building External Confidence

How the World Experiences You

**The world is full of potential friends
waiting for your energy to meet theirs.**

Chapter 9

The Power of Body Language and Presence

"You are always communicating—especially when you're silent."

Some people walk into a room, and without even trying, they make everyone feel at ease. It's not just how they look. It's something deeper, something unspoken.

If you met my friend Jeanine, you'd notice it instantly. She has that rare quality that makes people naturally gravitate toward her. Is it her smile? Absolutely. But it's also the way she carries herself: relaxed, confident, open, and always fully engaged in the moment. She listens intently, makes steady eye contact, and moves through the world with effortless warmth. Whether you've known her for years or you're meeting her for the first time, she makes you feel like you belong. Her presence feels effortless, and that's why people are drawn to her.

Of course, Jeanine is beautiful, and people notice her when she walks into a room. But what truly makes her unforgettable isn't just how she looks; it's how she makes people feel. She takes care of her appearance, but if you asked her about it, she'd just shrug and say, "My mother always said, when you look good, you feel good."

So, why am I telling you this? When it comes to how others perceive you, physical attractiveness isn't the most important factor. What truly matters is **how you feel on the inside and how you carry yourself on the outside**. That inner confidence—the ease, the openness, the ability to connect—is what genuinely attracts people. Even if Jeanine is in gym clothes with her hair in a messy bun, her warmth and approachable demeanor are enough to spark a conversation with a stranger in line at the grocery store.

Now, think about the opposite scenario. Have you ever interacted with someone who seemed closed off before they even spoke? Maybe they avoided eye contact, crossed their arms tightly, or kept their body turned slightly away. They weren't rude, but something about their posture made the conversation feel distant or awkward.

Which person would you rather talk to?

Some people just own the room the moment they walk in. There's something about them: their confidence, their ease, the way people naturally gravitate toward them. It's not just what they say, it's how they carry themselves, the silent signals they send without even realizing it. They have something, an undeniable presence, that natural likability.

Here's the best part: you can have it too.

THE POWER OF BODY LANGUAGE AND PRESENCE

Most of the time, we have no idea what we're silently communicating. You might feel totally confident on the inside, but if your posture is weak, your movements hesitant, or your gestures uncertain, that confidence isn't translating. Or maybe you have the opposite problem. You come across as too intense, too serious, or even intimidating without meaning to, making it harder to connect with people.

What if you could turn things around and create a cool first impression? What if you knew exactly how to send the right signals? Ones that make people instantly like, respect, and remember you? Imagine walking into a room and knowing you have that magnetic presence that draws people in.

That's where nonverbal communication becomes your secret superpower.

Over the years, researchers, therapists, and professionals across law enforcement, behavioral psychology, and even leadership coaching have studied what our body language says long before we open our mouths. And here's the surprising part: people don't just hear you, they feel you. The warmth in your smile. The confidence in your posture. The calm in your gaze. It all registers instantly, whether you're speaking to a friend, walking into a meeting, or standing in line at the grocery store.

And it's not about acting or pretending to be someone you're not. It's about learning how to align your physical presence with your inner self, so that people around you instinctively trust, connect, and respond.

You don't need to be a behavioral expert or a former agent to understand body language. You just need to know what to look for and how to carry yourself in a way that reflects who you really are. Let's start there.

Energy Speaks Before You Do

As we explore body language, remember this: **Your presence isn't about being perfect—it's about being aligned.** When your internal energy and external presence match, you show up as your best self: open, grounded, and naturally magnetic.

In earlier chapters, we explored the importance of balanced energy: the harmony between internal energy (your mindset and emotional state) and external energy (how you communicate with the world).

When your inner and outer energy are in sync, confidence flows naturally. But when they're out of alignment—when you feel anxious inside but try to fake confidence—others can feel the mismatch. The good news? You don't have to fake it. The idea is to shift your internal energy first, so your body language follows naturally. Think of your energy as having two layers:

1. **Internal Energy = Your Thoughts and Emotional State**
   (Am I feeling calm, grounded, and present? Or am I stuck in self-doubt?)
2. **External Energy = Your Body Language and Presence**
   (Am I carrying myself with openness, confidence, and ease? Or am I tense and withdrawn?)

Think about a time when you were nervous but tried to act confident. Maybe you overcompensated by laughing too loudly or freezing up completely, worried about saying the wrong thing. Even if people couldn't put their finger on it, they probably sensed something felt off. That's the disconnection between internal and external energy. This chapter builds on that foundation.

People aren't just listening to your words—they're reading your presence. Even before you speak, your body communicates your internal state. This is a form of *emotional contagion*—the subtle way your energy influences others without a word.

Joe Navarro, a former FBI body language expert, explains that when we meet someone new, we're not scanning for confidence—we're instinctively picking up on cues of comfort or discomfort:

- If your body language is open, relaxed, and aligned, people instinctively feel at ease around you.
- If you appear tense, hesitant, or closed off, people subconsciously mirror that discomfort.

This happens instantly, before anyone even registers the words you say. Your presence shifts the energy of a room before you even speak.

It's true. When you are tense or anxious, it makes others feel uncomfortable, even if you're trying your best to hide it. But when you are grounded, your presence puts people at ease because they can sense that you're comfortable in your own skin. Your body (your external presence) follows your thoughts (your internal energy).

> Instead of asking: "How do I look confident?"
> Ask: **"How do I feel confident?"**
> When you feel it first, the rest follows naturally.

Charlie: The Walk-In Moment

Charlie stood just outside his fifth-grade classroom, coffee in one hand, keys in the other. The school hallway was quiet, but his mind was anything but.

It was the first day back after winter break, and something about returning to routine always stirred up old feelings: *Will I connect with the new kids? Did I prep enough? Do I still sound like I know what I'm doing?*

He caught himself shrinking a little, shoulders tight, chest caved in, jaw clenched.

This time, instead of powering through, he paused. Right there outside the door.

He took a breath and silently ran through his new ritual:

- **Check in.** *What energy am I bringing in today? Am I calm? Anxious? Tense?*
- **Shift the body.** He loosened his shoulders, opened his stance, and softened his face.
- **Align.** *Speak clearly. Ground your voice. Look up. Let your posture reflect how you want to feel.*

Then he whispered a phrase he'd started carrying in his pocket for moments like this: **"You belong here."**

He opened the door, smiled, and greeted the first student walking in. It wasn't dramatic. He didn't feel amazing.

But he felt real. Present. Just enough.

The biggest lesson?
Your body follows your thoughts.

HOW YOU CAN DO IT

1. Check in with yourself before entering a social setting.
- How am I feeling right now?
- What energy am I bringing into this space?
- Am I present, or am I in my head?

2. Adjust your posture first.
- Stand tall, relax your shoulders, and take a deep breath.
- Let your body signal confidence before your mind catches up.

3. Use the power of a pause.
- Before speaking, take a beat to breathe instead of rushing.
- This simple act signals control and presence.

Your body shapes how you feel and how others see you.

Want to feel more confident? Start with your posture. It doesn't just reflect confidence. It builds it. Research on power posing (standing tall, with open, expansive posture) shows that holding a confident stance for just two minutes can literally change your brain chemistry, raising testosterone (the confidence hormone) and lowering cortisol (the stress hormone). Even if power poses don't radically shift hormones, they do shift self-perception.

People remember how you show up: your presence, your energy, and how you take up space. And the best part? You don't have to be loud or extroverted to have presence. You just need to show up fully, intentionally, and as yourself.

The Science of Likability and The Trust Triangle

First impressions happen fast, sometimes before you even speak. And those few seconds? They count.

What people are really scanning for isn't just your smile or handshake.

They're subconsciously asking: *Can I trust this person?*

That trust doesn't come from one single trait. It's a feeling shaped by what I call the **trust triangle**—a simple, powerful framework I use in my work with clients.

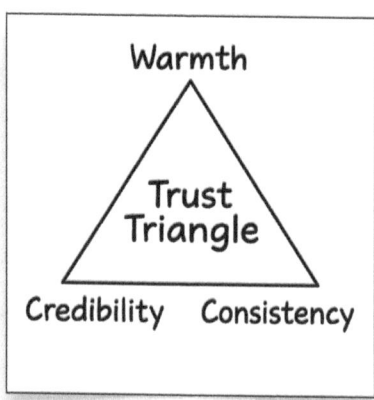

To build trust and likability, three things must be present:

1. **Warmth** – Do you seem kind, open, and emotionally safe to be around?
2. **Credibility** – Do you seem like you know what you're talking about (without being arrogant)?
3. **Consistency** – Do your words and energy match? Do you seem like someone who follows through?

When all three points of the triangle are aligned, people lean in. They listen. They feel safe enough to open up. But if one side is missing, trust wobbles, and connection can slip away.

Let's bring this idea to life with three familiar faces: Marina, Joe, and Charlie.

Marina: Warm, But Doubtful

Marina is the kind of person who makes people feel instantly seen. She compliments your earrings. She remembers your favorite coffee order. Her warmth is genuine and effortless.

But when it comes time to speak up, she freezes. She second-guesses her insights. Even when she's right on target, she might say, "This is probably a dumb idea, but…" Marina's warmth is front and center. But her credibility? She hides it.

As a result, people like her, but they don't always look to her for leadership or guidance. Her trust triangle is missing a key side.

Marina's Shift: When she started saying, "Here's one idea I've been thinking about," instead of apologizing for her voice, something changed. Her warmth never left. It grew stronger. And that strength earned respect.

Joe: Skilled, But Closed

Joe is brilliant, an analytical thinker, a master of systems. But when you meet him, he's reserved. Quiet. Sometimes even looks away during conversation.

He's not cold; he's cautious. But that's not how it always lands.

At a recent community meetup, a friend whispered to Marina, "I don't think Joe likes me." The truth? Joe was just overthinking his words and keeping his guard up. His credibility was strong, but warmth and consistency were missing.

Joe's Shift: When he started saying "Hi, I'm Joe" with a steady handshake and offering a lighthearted comment about traffic or music, people began to see his personality. His triangle started balancing out and was now approachable.

Charlie: Grounded, Open, and Trustworthy

Charlie walks into a room and doesn't demand attention, but people notice him anyway. He listens deeply, speaks clearly, and shares moments from his life that make others feel understood.

He asks real questions. He gives real answers. And he shows up the same whether he's talking to a neighbor, a boss, or a teenager.

Charlie's trust triangle is solid:
- His warmth comes through in his smile and openness.
- His credibility is quiet but undeniable.
- His consistency? Rock solid. He says what he means, and he means what he says.

Charlie's Edge: People trust Charlie not because he's flashy, but because he's congruent. There's no performance. Just presence.

You don't need to change who you are. You just need to notice how you're showing up. Here's a simple way to start aligning your presence with how you want to be experienced:

1. Identify Your Default Setting

Ask yourself: *When I meet new people, what do I naturally lead with?* Are you warm and friendly, but tend to downplay your knowledge? Or do you come across as confident and prepared, but struggle to show openness? Recognizing your natural baseline is the first step toward balance.

2. Strengthen Your Softer Side (Warmth)

If you tend to lead with logic, intellect, or authority, practice adding small signals of warmth. This could mean offering a genuine compliment, making eye contact, or smiling when you greet someone. Warmth isn't about putting on a bubbly personality. It's about showing up with openness and sincerity.

3. Own Your Strengths (Credibility)

If you tend to be more easygoing or self-deprecating, check in with your credibility. Are you downplaying your ideas? Do you rush to say, "I'm not an expert"? Practice standing behind your voice. Confidence doesn't need to shout. It just needs to be steady and grounded.

4. Align Your Energy (Consistency)

People trust what feels congruent. Does your body language match your words? Are you the same "you" in different settings? Take a moment to ground yourself before a conversation so you can show up centered, rather than scattered or "on." When your energy feels real, people know they can rely on you.

When your internal self matches your external cues—when people sense warmth, credibility, and consistency in how you carry yourself—they feel something solid. They trust you.

And trust is magnetic.

You don't need to fake anything or overhaul your personality. You just need to know where you naturally lean, and gently strengthen the parts that aren't being seen yet.

That's the power of the trust triangle.

Body Language
The Silent Language of Confidence

You've probably heard the saying, "Actions speak louder than words." But when it comes to confidence, influence, and connection, that's not just an expression, it's science.

Studies show that over 70% of communication is nonverbal, which means that before you even say a word, people are already forming an impression of you. Your posture, gestures, facial expressions, and eye contact send signals that tell others whether you're confident, nervous, approachable, or distant.

THE POWER OF BODY LANGUAGE AND PRESENCE

Your body speaks before you do.
Make sure it's saying what you want.

Think about it. Have you ever met someone who instantly felt like a leader without them even introducing themselves? Maybe it was the way they carried themselves, their calm and steady presence, or the way they looked people in the eye with ease. On the flip side, have you ever met someone who seemed uncertain, even before they spoke? Their hunched shoulders, fidgeting hands, or downward gaze made them seem unsure of themselves, even if they were highly intelligent or capable.

This is the power of **body language**.

Your physical presence has the ability to either reinforce your words or completely undermine them. You can be the most knowledgeable person in the room, but if your body language suggests hesitation, people will subconsciously doubt you. Conversely, you can say very little, yet exude confidence and trustworthiness simply by the way you stand, move, and engage with others.

Small shifts in posture, movement, and eye contact can make a huge difference in how people perceive you and how you feel about yourself. And here's where it gets interesting: **body language plays out differently in person vs. virtually**.

In face-to-face interactions, people can read your full-body presence, making posture, gestures, and spatial awareness incredibly important. In virtual settings, your upper body, facial expressions, and tone of voice become your primary tools for communication. Each setting requires different adjustments to ensure you're coming across the way you want to.

Let's break it down.

Own the Room Without Saying a Word

You don't need to speak to make a first impression because your body's already doing the talking.

Most of us walk into rooms without realizing we're already communicating. Our posture, our eye contact, the way we hold our shoulders or scan the room, it's all part of our unspoken presence. That's why it's so important to become aware of what your body might be saying, especially in social or professional settings where confidence matters.

But owning the room doesn't mean being the loudest or most outgoing. It simply means showing up in a way that aligns with your most grounded, connected self.

Here's how to begin.

1. Anchor Yourself With Posture

Think of your posture as your emotional anchor. When you stand tall, with your feet planted, shoulders relaxed, and spine straight, you show calm confidence to others. More importantly, it signals this to you. Studies have shown that just a few seconds of upright posture can shift your internal state, helping you feel more alert and empowered.

A client once told me, "When I uncrossed my arms and stopped hunching, I felt ten pounds lighter. I hadn't realized I was literally folding in on myself." That awareness was a turning point. Her body began doing what her words couldn't. It created connection.

2. Lead with Your Heart

There's a simple shift I teach that changes everything: imagine your chest—the center of your warmth and sincerity—leading your body as you walk or sit. Not your head. Not your hips. Your heart.

This gentle, invisible adjustment creates a subtle openness in your posture. You appear (and feel) more available, more centered, and more welcoming. Leading with your heart softens your edges without weakening your presence. It's a cue people instinctively respond to.

3. Use Your Eyes to Signal Presence

Eye contact is tricky. It's not about staring people down, but about creating shared space. Warm, steady eye contact signals: I see you. I'm here. I'm listening.

Try this: when entering a room, make brief, relaxed eye contact with one or two people. Smile softly. Even a three-second connection can shift how approachable you appear and how connected you feel.

For those who feel shy or socially anxious, this can feel intimidating. But think of your eyes as a soft light, not a spotlight. You're not performing. You're connecting.

4. Own the Corners of the Room

One subtle trick that helps you appear grounded: expand your awareness. Don't just look straight ahead. Instead, notice the whole room. People who feel confident tend to "own" their space by gently scanning and making micro-adjustments to how they carry themselves within it.

If you walk in rushed or hunched, people read that as unease. But when you enter slowly, breathe, and claim your space, even silently, others take notice.

5. Let Your Hands Speak Calmly

Ever notice how someone's hands tell you more than their words? Hands that fidget, pick at clothing, or stay hidden in pockets often reveal nervous energy. But when hands are visible, calm, and intentional—resting gently on a table, loosely clasped, or used subtly when speaking—they signal steadiness.

Let your hands support what you're saying, not fight against it. Open palms. Unrushed movements. Stillness when needed. Body language is an invitation.

Owning the room isn't about being the most extroverted person there. It's about being in sync with yourself. When your body language aligns with your intention, and your energy is calm, open, and present, people feel it.

They don't need you to be perfect.
They just need to feel safe with you.
And that begins before you ever say a word.

Feeling Seen and Confident on Video Calls

There's something uniquely awkward about seeing your own face while trying to have a meaningful conversation.

Video calls have become a part of everyday life: from work meetings to virtual therapy to reconnecting with friends. But showing up on screen can trigger all kinds of unexpected insecurities. Suddenly, you're hyperaware of how your face looks, how your voice sounds, whether your background is tidy, or if your camera angle is unflattering. And that internal distraction? It can block a connection before the call even begins.

But video calls don't have to feel stiff or staged. With a few subtle shifts in presence, you can build the same kind of trust and warmth through a screen as you would across a table.

Here's how to carry your in-person energy into the virtual world without performing or overthinking it.

1. Frame Yourself Like a Pro (Without Being Perfect)

Think of your video frame as a window into your energy. You don't need a high-tech setup or fancy lighting. Just a clear, centered view of your face, at eye level. This simple adjustment makes you feel more grounded and more trustworthy to the person on the other side of the screen.

Too low, and it can feel like you're looking up at people. Too high, and you disappear. Aim to center your head and shoulders so your presence fills the screen naturally, like you're sitting across from someone, not floating below their desk.

And remember: clutter distracts. If your background is busy or messy, it pulls attention away from your message. A clean wall, plant, or shelf works fine. The goal isn't perfection. It's focus.

2. Master Virtual Eye Contact (Yes, It's Weird)

Here's the secret to feeling present on video: Look at the camera, not yourself.

It's tempting to check your own face throughout the call, especially if you're feeling nervous. But doing so shifts your energy inward. You become more self-conscious, and the connection gets diluted.

Instead, try this: whenever you're listening or speaking, glance at the camera lens like it's the other person's eyes. You don't need to stare, but a few steady seconds of camera-facing eye contact go a long way in building trust.

Tip: If it helps, place a tiny sticky note next to your webcam with a smiley face or the word "connect" to draw your attention upward.

3. Let Your Voice Carry Warmth

In virtual settings, tone does even more heavy lifting than usual. Since our bodies are less visible, people rely more on how we sound to interpret meaning.

To come across as approachable, try softening your tone just a bit. Slow your pace. Pause. Let your voice have range. It doesn't mean you need to sound fake-cheerful. It just means letting your real energy be heard.

I tell clients: Imagine you're talking to someone who's a little nervous. Speak in a way that helps them relax, and chances are, you'll start relaxing too.

4. Use Your Hands (Even On Screen)

Just because you're on video doesn't mean you have to stay perfectly still. In fact, small, visible hand gestures during video calls signal authenticity. They help reinforce what you're saying and show that you're present, not rehearsed.

Keep your hands where they can be seen occasionally, especially when you're making a point. A simple nod, a visible smile, or a light hand gesture all add texture to your presence and humanize the screen-to-screen interaction.

5. Mind Your Energy, Not Just Your Appearance

You can wear the perfect shirt, have the best lighting, and still come across as distant if your energy isn't there.

Before hopping on a video call, take 30 seconds to center yourself. Breathe. Ground your feet. Remind yourself of your intention: *To connect, not perform.*

One of my clients, who dreaded Zoom meetings, started practicing a short phrase before each call: "Let them see the real me." That mantra shifted her from self-monitoring to self-anchoring. And it changed everything about how she showed up.

It might seem like a screen creates distance, but in many ways, people are more tuned in than ever. They're watching your eyes, your voice, your pauses. They're feeling for presence.

You don't have to be perfect on video. Just be present. That's what makes people feel like you're truly there with them.

And presence, even through a screen, is powerful.

Decode Other People's Body Language

Most of us aren't taught how to read body language; we're just expected to "get it." But interpreting the signals others send, especially in high-stakes or emotionally charged situations, is a skill you can absolutely learn. And the better you get at reading people, the more you'll notice opportunities to respond with empathy, clarity, and confidence. But here's the key: **you're not looking for one single signal, you're looking for patterns.**

One gesture might mean a dozen different things, depending on the context. That's why I encourage clients to think of body language like a story: you're not reading one word, you're reading whole paragraphs. When you slow down, stay curious, and observe the full picture, people become much easier to understand. Here's how to begin decoding the people around you, without making assumptions or jumping to conclusions.

1. Look for Clusters, Not Clues

Imagine someone crosses their arms. Does that mean they're closed off? Not necessarily. They could be cold, tired, or simply comfortable that way. But if their arms are crossed, they're avoiding eye contact, their feet are angled away from you, and they're barely responding? We call that a cluster, a group of signals that often means someone is disengaged or uncomfortable. That's what you want to tune into: clusters of cues, not isolated movements.

Train yourself to take a step back mentally. Observe the big picture instead of fixating on a single action. People are full of nuance, and reading them well starts with assuming there's more beneath the surface.

2. Notice Shifts, Not Just States

We often focus too much on how someone looks, whether tense, relaxed, or cheerful, but what matters more is how they shift. A sudden change in posture, blinking rate, tone, or facial expression can reveal more than a fixed emotion.

Let's say someone is nodding while you speak, but suddenly stiffens when a certain topic comes up. Or they've been making eye contact, but glance away and fidget when asked a direct question. These micro-shifts matter. They're invitations to pause, reframe, or check in.

I've had clients realize in real time that their partner wasn't upset. They were simply overwhelmed and didn't know how to express it. It was the change in body language, not the posture itself, that told the truth.

3. Start With the Face, But Don't Stop There

We naturally look at faces first, and that's smart. Our faces hold emotional data, especially the microexpressions that flash across someone's eyes or mouth before they compose themselves. A quick lift of the eyebrows can signal surprise or disbelief. A tight jaw may indicate suppressed frustration.

But faces are also where people often mask their emotions. That's why it's important to also observe the whole body. Do their gestures match their words? Is their tone in sync with their expression? Does their overall body support or contradict what they're saying?

For example, someone might say, "I'm fine," while their shoulders are hunched and their voice has gone flat. The words say one thing, but the body says something else entirely.

These tiny facial cues often flash across someone's face in less than a second, but they can speak volumes. Once you learn to spot them, you start to see the feelings behind the words. Here's a quick reference of some of the most common microexpressions and what they may indicate:

KEY MICROEXPRESSIONS AND THEIR MEANINGS

Tight lips, furrowed brows	→ Suppressed frustration or disagreement
Raised eyebrows, slightly open mouth	→ Surprise or mild shock
One-sided smirk	→ Contempt or hidden amusement
Eye roll or exaggerated blink	→ Annoyance or impatience
Genuine smile (reaches the eyes)	→ Real enjoyment or connection

4. Watch the Feet (Really)

Feet are honest. While we're often self-conscious about our hands or faces, we rarely think about what our feet are doing. That's why they tend to reveal what someone really wants.

If a person's feet are pointed toward the door while you're talking, they may be looking for an exit, physically or emotionally. If their feet shift toward you during a conversation, even if their body remains still, that's often a subtle cue of increased trust or interest.

Paying attention to foot placement gives you data that others aren't thinking to manage or mask.

5. Energy Speaks Louder Than Expression

Sometimes the most powerful body language isn't visible, it's felt.

That shift in energy when someone walks into a room and suddenly the mood changes? That's body language too. It's posture, breathing, facial tension, eye movement, and presence, all wrapped together into what we perceive as a vibe or a charge.

One of my clients once said, "I didn't hear her say anything rude, but it felt like she didn't want me there." That feeling came from the woman's closed shoulders, lack of acknowledgment, and quick glances toward the clock. Those are the invisible cues that create emotional clarity, even when words don't.

When decoding others, listen to that felt sense. Your nervous system is often better at reading people than your brain is.

The goal of reading body language isn't to catch someone or label them. It's to understand so you can connect better, respond more clearly, and navigate tension with grace.

People aren't puzzles to solve. They're nervous systems trying to stay safe. When you read others with curiosity and care, you don't just see them more clearly, you help them feel seen too.

What to Take With You

A Quick Recap of Presence, Trust, and Body Language

You don't need to perform to make an impression. You don't need to be extroverted to be memorable. You just need to show up in a way that reflects who you really are.

When your body language, energy, and expression align with your intention, people feel it. They trust you, not because you're perfect, but because you're real.

Here's what to keep in mind as you carry these tools into your everyday presence:

Strengthen Your Trust Triangle

- Lead with **warmth**: a calm smile, steady tone, and soft eye contact go further than you think.
- Show your **credibility** by standing behind your words and presence, without needing to overprove.
- Build **consistency** by making sure your energy, actions, and words all tell the same story. People trust what feels congruent.

In-Person Body Language
- Anchor yourself with posture: grounded feet, open shoulders, and a soft face.
- Let your heart lead, not your head or shoulders, when you walk or speak.
- Use your eyes to create a connection, not control. Just a few moments of steady, warm eye contact can transform a moment.
- Own the space around you with relaxed movement and grounded awareness.
- Keep your hands visible and calm; they speak even when you don't.

On Video Calls
- Frame yourself at eye level so others feel like they're across from you, not looking down at you.
- Look at the camera, not your own face. Even brief camera-facing eye contact builds trust.
- Let your voice carry warmth by slowing your pace and softening your tone.
- Use small hand gestures and expressions to signal presence and realness.
- Ground yourself before the call so your energy, not just your image, comes through.

Decoding Others with Compassion
- Don't read a single signal, look for clusters of cues.
- Watch for shifts, not just states. What changes when a sensitive topic comes up?

- Start with the face, but trust the whole body to tell the full story.
- Yes, even the feet offer insight. Where they point reveals attention and interest.
- Trust your felt sense. Energy speaks, even when words are polished. If it feels off, pause. Stay curious.

Whether you're walking into a room, logging onto a screen, or quietly observing someone across the table, your presence sets the tone. And so does theirs. This chapter focuses on awareness, alignment, and authenticity. It's about learning to carry yourself like someone who already belongs—because you do.

You don't have to become someone else to be magnetic. You already have everything you need. Let your energy match your intention. Let your posture carry your presence. Let your kindness and confidence hold equal space.

What This Means: Your body is always speaking even before you do. The way you carry yourself, the energy you bring into a room, and the way you look at someone when they speak, these cues either build trust or create distance. Presence isn't about performing or posturing. It's about alignment. When warmth, credibility, and consistency show up together, people don't just see you. They feel you. And that's what makes the difference.

Why It Matters: In a world full of noise, authenticity stands out. We're all wired to read between the lines, to sense the story beneath the words. When your presence reflects your true self, you don't have to work as hard to connect or be heard. People lean in because something about you feels solid and safe. That's what opens doors, deepens relationships, and brings ease to your world, both online and in person.

What Comes Next: Start noticing how you show up, before the words even leave your mouth. Choose one setting this week where you can experiment with grounded posture, warmer tone, or steadier eye contact. Don't overthink it. Just let yourself be felt.

The more you embody your energy with intention, the more people will experience the version of you that's already trustworthy, already present, and already enough.

This is a practice I use myself before every talk, every session, every group I lead, and it works. So start small. Just shift your posture. Let people feel the real you.

> *"The way you carry yourself*
> *is the way you feel about yourself."*
>
> — *Tara Stiles*

Chapter 10

How You Make Them Feel Matters Most

"I've learned that people will forget what you said, people will forget what you did, but people will never forget how you made them feel."
— Maya Angelou

The Quietest Kind of Connection

Some people have a presence that doesn't fill a room— it settles it. They don't need the right words or the perfect tone. Something about the way they show up makes others feel safe. This chapter will guide you through the invisible art of connection. An art I learned not through speaking, but by sitting in silence with a grieving mother.

We'd never met before. A mutual friend had asked if I would visit her. She had just lost her daughter.

I wasn't a therapist then. I wasn't even sure I was the right person to go. But something in me said yes, maybe because I was a mother too. Maybe because I couldn't stop thinking about her pain.

When I arrived, she greeted me with a quiet grace. Her eyes were tired. Her movements were gentle, but heavy. Eventually, it was just the two of us alone in her small living room. No translator. No plan.

We sat side by side on her couch, knees nearly touching, and after a few minutes of silence, she placed a thick photo album in her lap. She opened it slowly, carefully. The pages were worn at the corners. Each turn revealed another glimpse into her daughter's life: birthday parties, playground smiles, dress-up days, and messy hair.

She didn't speak much. She didn't have to. I watched as her fingers lingered on each photo. As her face shifted, smiling at one memory, tearing up at the next. At some point, I realized we were holding hands. And then I felt it.

Not just sadness. Not just compassion. But something deeper. A profound, wordless alignment between two mothers, one holding onto memories, the other holding space. Two women, strangers in every outward way, suddenly sharing something unspeakably human.

I had shown up unsure and insecure, worried I might not have anything to offer. But she—she had shown up in her grief. And that takes more courage than I can begin to describe.

In that quiet, sacred space, I realized something powerful: Genuine connection often transcends words. The deepest comfort we can offer is not always in what we say, but in how we allow ourselves to truly feel with someone else. It's this invisible yet deeply impactful art, the art of making others feel truly understood, that we'll explore together in this chapter.

That quiet moment in her living room never left me. It was sacred in its stillness, just two mothers, two nervous systems, present with one another in the rawest way. But presence isn't limited to private spaces. Not long after, I found myself in a moment that looked completely different—public, exposed, overwhelming—but somehow carried the same invitation:

Be real. Be there. Let your energy do the work.

A Different Kind of Courage

Some of the most powerful moments I've had with other people have nothing to do with words. They're the quiet exchanges: the look across a room, the shift in someone's posture, the unspoken understanding that passes between two nervous systems.

I was standing in the cafeteria of a local elementary school around 7 p.m., about to speak to a room full of parents, teachers, and staff. We were gathered to talk about radKIDS, a personal empowerment and safety program I was introducing to the community, with the hope of enrolling students into the upcoming class.

It was a big group, about fifty adults, spread out at five or six long tables, seated in the front half of the room closest to me. Everyone looked tired. I felt it too. We were all coming off long days: working parents, the school principal, and me included.

The fluorescent lights felt a little too bright. The room still smelled faintly of chicken nuggets. And I was suddenly hyperaware of how flat my voice sounded through the glitchy microphone. I could feel myself gripping the sides of the mic a little too tightly as I tried to keep the energy up, trying to be engaging while wondering if anyone even wanted to be there.

That's when I made a choice. I set the mic down and stopped pretending it was working. Then I turned around, stepped up onto the stage behind me, not to elevate myself, but to be seen and heard. I sat on the edge of the stage and projected my voice as best I could, making eye contact with the adults in front of me, speaking from the part of me that actually believed in what I was saying.

Then the room shifted. Not in any obvious way, no applause or major moment. Just a subtle recalibration of energy. A new kind of focus. And that's when I saw her... sitting at the end of one of the tables, arms folded, head tilted slightly.

She hadn't said a word. Her face was unreadable. Not closed, exactly, just distant. But when our eyes met for a brief second, something softened. Her posture shifted just slightly. And I could feel it, not just from her, but from the entire room. That tiny change in the atmosphere you only notice when you're paying attention.

Afterward, as people began gathering their things and filtering out of the cafeteria, she approached me. Her movements were tentative, careful. She only said one simple sentence.

"I don't speak much English," she said. "But I felt what you meant. I understood."

I nodded, not sure what to say in return, but feeling everything. It wasn't about the clarity of my words. It wasn't about the presentation going smoothly.

What stayed with me was that quiet, shared pause between us. The way something unspoken passed between two people from different lives, different languages, in the middle of a fluorescent-lit cafeteria at the end of a long day.

Confidence isn't about how you feel about yourself—
it's about how you make others feel in your presence.
When you trust yourself, people trust you.
When you are at ease, others feel safe around you.

Cultivating the Confidence to Make Others Feel Safe and Understood

If you've ever been around someone who was completely at ease with themselves, you've likely felt more relaxed in their presence. There's something calming about being with people who aren't trying too hard, aren't anxious about how they're coming across, and aren't caught up in their own insecurities.

That's because confidence signals emotional safety. It's an unspoken message that tells others: You don't have to perform here. You can just be yourself.

But here's where many people go wrong: They think confidence is about them. They think it's about appearing impressive, polished, or in control. But true confidence, the kind that creates connection, isn't about proving anything. It's about making others feel comfortable, valued, and at ease.

For many of us, mental habits like self-doubt, overthinking, and hesitation can quietly chip away at our presence. We become so focused on getting it right that we disconnect from how we actually feel. But when we start to shift those patterns even slightly we show up differently. More grounded. More attuned. And when that shift happens? People feel it immediately. That shift is what allows us to radiate ease, focus outward, and truly show up for others.

Radiate Confidence That Puts Others at Ease

We tend to think of confidence as something we project outward, but the truth is, **confidence is felt by others before it's ever seen.**

Think about the last time you met someone who carried themselves with quiet confidence. Maybe they weren't the loudest in the room, but something about them made you feel comfortable, even safe. Their presence was steady, warm, and open, and because of that, you felt more at ease.

Now think of the opposite, someone who tried too hard, constantly sought approval, or carried subtle nervous energy. You likely felt a little uneasy around them, even if they were friendly. Why? Because we pick up on unspoken signals.

Confidence isn't about being dominant, charismatic, or in control. It's about creating a sense of calm, openness, and warmth that makes people feel like they can let their guard down.

I remember the first time I walked into a new class where I didn't know anyone. My brain immediately started the usual script: *Everyone already knows each other. They probably think I don't belong. What if I say something weird?*

I caught myself mid-thought and reminded myself: *Confidence isn't about making people like you. It's about making them feel comfortable.*

So instead of trying to impress, I focused on being open and at ease. I smiled at the first person I made eye contact with. I asked someone a simple question about the class. I didn't try to be interesting. I just showed up present and engaged.

By the end of the class, I wasn't on the outside looking in. I was part of the group. Not because I had been charming or impressive, but because I had shown up in a way that made others feel comfortable around me.

Confidence is never about you. It's about what your presence allows others to feel.

Shift Attention to Others Instead of Worrying About Yourself

One of the biggest obstacles to connection is that we're too focused on ourselves.

Remember that time you walked into a party or gathering and immediately thought *People are noticing how awkward I look? They can probably tell I don't belong here. I should have stayed home.*

The spotlight effect tricks us into thinking people are paying much more attention to us than they really are. That fact is, most people aren't analyzing you nearly as much as you imagine. Like you, they're caught up in their own thoughts, often focused on their own insecurities. But when you shift your attention outward—when you stop worrying about how you're being perceived and start focusing on helping others feel at ease—you naturally become more confident, more present, and more engaging.

I remember being invited to a birthday party for a friend, and I only knew one person there. At first, I hung back and worried about how I appeared to everyone. Then I thought, what if I stopped focusing on myself and instead made it all about celebrating them?

So I turned my attention outward. I noticed someone standing alone and struck up a simple conversation: "How do you know the host?" A few minutes later, I was in the middle of an easy conversation. Not because I had made a great impression, but because I had stopped worrying about making an impression at all.

Confidence isn't about thinking highly of yourself.
It's about thinking less about yourself, so you can be fully present for the people in front of you.

Release Old Beliefs to Show Up Fully

Sometimes, the biggest thing holding us back from connection isn't what's happening now, but what happened in the past.

Maybe at some point, you were made to feel like your voice didn't matter. Maybe you were criticized for being too much or not enough. Or maybe you internalized the idea that people don't really care what you have to say.

I remember many years ago, sitting alone at a friend's birthday dinner at a restaurant. I didn't know most of the people at the table, and as conversations bubbled around me, I felt myself shrink back. Everyone seemed to have a shared history, inside jokes, and easy banter.

I smiled politely and nodded, but inside, the old belief crept in: *You're not interesting enough to join in. You'll just say something awkward. Better to stay quiet.*

So I did. For most of the evening, I sat silently, feeling more invisible with every course.

But halfway through dessert, something shifted. One of the guests mentioned *Law & Order*, and I decided to speak up. Just one small comment—"I swear, I've seen that episode like five times and I still get chills."

To my surprise, it sparked a lively back-and-forth. Others chimed in, and suddenly, I was part of the conversation.

The truth was, no one was judging me. I had judged myself before anyone else had the chance.

So much of what holds us back in relationships isn't real. It's a belief we accepted at some point. And the moment we let go of those outdated narratives, we create space for something new: genuine, effortless connection.

Final Thoughts on Confidence and Connection

The way you feel about yourself isn't just about you. It's about how others experience you.

- When you trust yourself, people trust you.
- When you're at ease, people feel safe around you.

- When you stop focusing on yourself, you make space for real connection.

Confidence is about making others feel comfortable, valued, and seen. So the next time you find yourself hesitating, wondering if you belong, if you're being judged, or if you're saying the right thing, remind yourself:

People may forget your words, but they'll never forget how you made them feel. And how you make them feel starts with how you show up—fully, openly, and at ease.

HOW YOU CAN DO IT

MAKE OTHERS FEEL SAFE AND UNDERSTOOD

✔ **Radiate confidence that puts others at ease.**
Trust yourself so that people feel safe around you. Confidence isn't about proving something—it's about creating a space where others feel comfortable.

✔ **Shift attention to others vs. worrying about yourself.**
People aren't analyzing you as much as you think they are. Focus on making them feel valued, and a connection will happen naturally

✔ **Release old beliefs to show up fully.**
Identify an old belief that is holding you back in relationships.
Ask yourself: Is this really true? Challenge the story and replace it with one that supports who you're becoming.

The way you feel about yourself directly impacts how you make others feel in your presence.

Active Listening Is Your Gateway to Connection

We've all been in conversations where we could tell the other person wasn't really listening. Maybe they were nodding along while glancing at their phone. Maybe they interrupted mid-sentence to share their own similar story. Or maybe they responded with something that made it clear they weren't tuned in at all.

And then, there are conversations where we feel deeply heard, where the person in front of us is fully present, engaged, and genuinely interested. Those are the moments that build trust, connection, and understanding.

Active listening isn't about hearing someone's words. It's about making them feel seen and valued. It's the difference between casual interaction and meaningful connection.

But here's the challenge: Most of us think we're good listeners. The truth? We're not. In everyday conversations, most people are either:

1. Waiting for their turn to speak instead of truly listening.
2. Mentally crafting their response instead of being present.
3. Filtering what they hear through their own experiences instead of fully receiving the other person's perspective.

It's not that we don't care. It's that we were never taught how to listen in a way that makes people feel understood.

"Listening isn't about waiting for your turn to speak. It's about making someone feel truly heard."

I once read something in a magazine about friendship that stuck with me. It said that when someone you care about is going through a hard time, like losing a job, the most supportive thing you can do is simple: **ask how they're doing, and then stop talking**. Just be quiet. Listen.

We often think we're being relatable by jumping in with our own story: "That happened to me once," or "I've been thinking about quitting too," or "When my sister lost her job…" But as well-meaning as it may be, those moments can unintentionally shift the focus away from your friend and onto you. It's no longer about their pain. Now, it's your story.

Instead, try asking gentle questions about them:

"How are you feeling today?"

"What's been the hardest part?"

"What do you need right now?"

It's not about having the perfect words. It's about showing up in a way that reminds them: *I'm here for you. This moment is still yours.* Listening isn't about waiting for your turn to speak. It's about making someone feel truly heard.

What Does Active Listening Actually Look Like?

Active listening is more than just hearing words. It's about engaging with someone's emotions, thoughts, and experiences in a way that makes them feel truly valued.

It looks like:

- Being fully present (not distracted by your phone, your own thoughts, or external noise).
- Responding with curiosity instead of assumptions.

- Validating emotions before jumping to solutions.
- Listening for what's not being said, reading between the lines.

When done well, active listening creates trust, diffuses conflict, and makes others feel safe opening up to you.

But the best way to understand active listening isn't through a list of strategies. It's through a story.

Holly and Ryan's Story

Holly and Ryan had been together for years, but lately, their conversations felt more like surface-level exchanges than real communication.

One evening, Ryan came home from work, visibly tense. As they sat down for dinner, Holly could tell something was off.

"You okay?" she asked.

"Yeah, just tired," Ryan muttered, barely making eye contact.

Holly sighed. This was becoming a pattern. Whenever Ryan seemed stressed, he shut down. And whenever she asked what was wrong, he brushed it off. She felt like she was trying to connect, but he was pulling away.

Holly meant well. She thought that sharing her own stress might make Ryan feel less alone.

"Well, work's been insane for me too," she said, frustration creeping into her voice. "I barely had time to eat today."

But Ryan just nodded absentmindedly, not really responding. The conversation stalled.

She realized what she was doing: relating by comparison, not by connection.

So instead of withdrawing, she took a breath and softened.

"Hey... I feel like something's really bothering you. You don't have to tell me everything, but I just want you to know I'm here. You don't have to carry it alone."

Ryan looked up. For the first time that night, his expression softened.

"It's just work," he admitted. "I got blamed for something I didn't even do, and I know I shouldn't care so much, but it just got to me today."

Holly resisted the urge to offer solutions or compare it to her own stress. Instead, she leaned in.

"That sounds awful. That must've been so frustrating."

Ryan exhaled, like he had been holding something in all day.

"Yeah... it really was."

For the first time in weeks, Ryan felt like Holly really saw him, not just his words, but his emotions. And because of that, he opened up.

That night, their conversation didn't end in silence or frustration. It ended with understanding. And all it took was listening with presence and empathy.

Final Thoughts on Active Listening

The fastest way to deepen any relationship—whether it's with a partner, a friend, a coworker, or a stranger—is to listen in a way that makes them feel truly heard. People don't open up because you force them to talk. They open up because they feel safe enough to share. And that safety? It starts with how well you listen.

> **HOW YOU CAN DO IT**
>
> Active listening is about creating a space where people feel safe to express themselves.
>
> ✔ **Resisting the urge to relate or fix things right away.**
>
> Instead of responding with "I totally get it, I had a tough day too," pause and focus on them first.
>
> ✔ **Naming the emotion before offering advice.**
>
> "That sounds frustrating," or "I can see why that would be so stressful."
>
> ✔ **Asking open-ended questions that invite deeper conversation.**
>
> Instead of "Are you okay?" try "What's been on your mind lately?"
>
> **When you listen without judgment or distraction, you make people feel like they matter. And that's the foundation of every meaningful connection.**

Navigating Challenging Personalities

Not everyone we interact with will be easy to get along with. We've all had conversations that left us drained, frustrated, or unsure of how to respond. Some people interrupt constantly, others dominate conversations, and some shut down completely.

The reality is, you can't change other people's personalities, but you can change how you respond to them. Instead of avoiding difficult conversations or letting them frustrate us, we can learn how to navigate challenging personalities in a way that builds connection rather than deepens disconnection.

When you approach difficult people with understanding instead of resistance, you gain the ability to guide the conversation in a way that strengthens, not strains, your relationships.

> Some people challenge us, but every interaction is an opportunity to build a connection.

People communicate in vastly different ways. Some are naturally outgoing and expressive, while others are reserved. Some thrive on debate and discussion, while others avoid conflict at all costs. Learning to recognize different personalities and adjusting how we interact with them can make all the difference. Let's look at a few common personality types that can be challenging and how to navigate them.

1. The Over-Talker: Someone Who Dominates the Conversation

The Challenge: This person loves to talk. They may jump from one topic to the next without pausing, rarely giving you a chance to speak. Conversations with them can feel like a one-sided monologue.

Mia was at a friend's dinner party...

She was introduced to Caleb. Within minutes, Caleb launched into an energetic monologue about his latest business venture. Mia tried to interject a few times, but Caleb barely acknowledged her input before continuing his train of thought.

By the end of the conversation, Mia realized she had barely spoken at all. She felt invisible. Frustrated. Like she could have slipped away from the table, and no one would've noticed.

How to Handle It:

Instead of waiting for a natural pause (which might never come), try using a graceful interruption:

- "That's really interesting, Caleb! It reminds me of something I wanted to ask you…"
- "I love that point. Let me add to that before I forget…"

People like Caleb don't always realize they're dominating the conversation. Redirecting with a gentle yet assertive approach helps balance the interaction.

2. The Closed-Off Communicator: Someone Who Avoids Opening Up

The Challenge: This person keeps conversations short and doesn't easily share their thoughts or emotions. They often give one-word answers and avoid personal topics.

Lena started a new job…

She wanted to build a friendly connection with her coworker, Jake. Every time she asked him how his weekend was, he would respond with a simple, "Good."

After a few weeks, she felt like she was hitting a brick wall. She began to wonder if she was doing something wrong or if Jake just wasn't interested in connecting.

How to Handle It:

Some people aren't naturally talkative, but that doesn't mean they don't want to connect. It just means they might need a different approach.

Instead of asking general questions like "How was your weekend?" try something more specific and open-ended:

- "Did you do anything fun over the weekend?"
- "What's been keeping you busy lately?"
- "If you could take a month off work, where would you go?"

One Monday, she gave it a shot: "What's one show you could rewatch over and over again?"

Jake didn't hesitate. "Oh, definitely *Breaking Bad*," he said, laughing. For the first time, Lena saw a real spark.

That one small shift—asking a more engaging, open-ended question—helped break the surface-level interactions and start a real conversation.

3. The Contrarian: Someone Who Always Plays Devil's Advocate

The Challenge: This person seems to thrive on disagreement. No matter what you say, they counter it with an opposing point of view. They may think they're being thought-provoking, but in reality, their constant need to challenge can be exhausting.

Mark went to a family gathering…

He made a simple comment about how much he enjoyed a recent book. His cousin Victor immediately chimed in:

"Really? I thought it was totally overrated. The writing wasn't that great."

Mark sighed. This wasn't the first time Victor had done this. It felt like every sentence was a setup for an argument he didn't sign up for. No matter the topic, he always had an opposite opinion to share.

How to Handle It:

Instead of getting defensive or trying to "win" the discussion, acknowledge their perspective without feeding the debate:

- "That's an interesting take. I can see why you'd feel that way."
- "I get that. I personally loved it, but I appreciate hearing another perspective."

When you stop engaging in back-and-forth arguments, people like Victor often lose interest in debating because they're not getting the reaction they expect.

Mark tried this approach at the next gathering, and to his surprise, the conversation didn't turn into an argument. It simply moved on.

4. The Emotional Reactor: Someone Who Responds Strongly to Everything

The Challenge: This person experiences intense emotional reactions, such as anger, frustration, or defensiveness, even over minor things. They may take things personally, escalate conflicts quickly, or struggle to remain calm during discussions.

David had a coworker...

Angela would get visibly upset whenever someone gave her constructive feedback. Even small suggestions, like changing the formatting of a document, would result in her shutting down or becoming defensive.

David started censoring himself, not because the feedback wasn't important, but because he didn't know how to offer it without triggering a meltdown.

Over time, he found himself avoiding giving her any feedback, which created tension in their working relationship.

How to Handle It:

With emotionally reactive people, the key is to stay calm and not match their energy.

Acknowledge their feelings without escalating the situation:

- "I can see this is really frustrating for you."
- "I hear you. I know this isn't what you were expecting."

Set clear, neutral boundaries:

- "I want to work through this together. Let's take a minute and figure out what would help."

David started adjusting how he gave feedback to Angela, focusing on positive reinforcement first and framing changes as a collaborative effort. Over time, she became more receptive because she no longer felt attacked.

Bottom Line on Navigating Challenging Personalities

Difficult conversations don't have to drain you. They can actually help you connect better.

- The **Over-Talker** may just need gentle redirection.

- The **Closed-Off Communicator** may need the right question to open up.
- The **Contrarian** may lose interest when they're not given a debate.
- The **Emotional Reactor** may just need to feel heard before they can calm down.

The more you learn to navigate different personalities, the easier it becomes to build connections even with people who challenge you. Because connection is about learning how to meet people where they are and create understanding, no matter who you're talking to.

HOW YOU CAN DO IT

✔ **Recognize that difficult personalities aren't personal.**
People aren't trying to be difficult. This is just how they communicate.

✔ **Use curiosity instead of defensiveness.**
Instead of reacting emotionally, try to understand where they're coming from.

✔ **Know when to engage and when to let go.**
Not every conversation needs to be won. Sometimes, the best strategy is to redirect, defuse, or move on.

✔ **Set boundaries with kindness.**
Being kind doesn't mean being a doormat. You can stay firm while still being respectful.

The Lasting Impact of How You Make Others Feel

Think back to the most meaningful conversations you've ever had. The ones that left an imprint on your heart. Maybe it was a moment where someone truly listened to you, where you felt understood in a way that words couldn't fully capture. Or maybe it was an unexpected connection, a brief but powerful interaction that stayed with you long after it ended.

Now think about the opposite, the times when a conversation left you feeling invisible, unheard, or dismissed.

The difference between these experiences isn't about what was said. It's about how you felt in that moment.

That's the essence of human connection.

We spend so much time worrying about saying the right thing, but in reality, what matters most is how we show up.

- Are we fully present in our interactions, or are we distracted by our own thoughts and insecurities?
- Do we make people feel safe and valued, or do we leave them feeling unheard?
- Are we bringing ease and warmth into conversations, or are we unknowingly making them feel tense or defensive?

The way you make others feel is your legacy in every interaction. And the best part? You don't have to be perfect to leave a positive impact. You just have to be intentional.

Because when you make people feel seen, heard, and valued, you don't just improve relationships. You transform them.

What This Means: Whether you're sitting beside someone in silence or standing in front of a crowd, what people remember most isn't your title, your polish, or even your words. It's your presence. It's the way your energy meets theirs: grounded, real, and human. True connection isn't something you perform; it's something you allow. And when you're fully there, with your fear, your care, and your heart wide open, people feel it. And they trust it.

Why It Matters: In a world filled with noise, urgency, and shallow interactions, being someone who makes others feel safe is rare and powerful. You don't have to have all the answers. You don't need a perfect plan or the right script. You just need to show up with your nervous system settled, your mind quiet, and your presence intact. That's what creates emotional safety. That's what makes someone feel truly seen.

What Comes Next: Practice presence, not performance. The next time you're with someone, whether in a meeting, a moment of grief, or an everyday conversation, ask yourself: Can they feel me here with them?

Breathe. Ground. Let your energy speak. The feeling you leave behind might just become the part of you they remember most.

Become the kind of person
who makes a room feel a little lighter.
A little more human. A little safer.

Chapter 11

Say Hello First: The Art of Starting a Conversation

"A simple hello could lead to a million things."

I don't remember what I ate that day, but I do remember the regret. Not a big, life-changing kind of regret—just that nagging little pinch from not saying hello. I was meeting my friend Natalie at a new restaurant we'd both been excited to try. I actually showed up early, which never happens, and ended up sitting alone at our table for two. That's when it happened. A chance to start a conversation with someone new. And I let it slip by.

It had been a while since I'd gone out to lunch with anyone, and I made a conscious effort to resist the urge to scroll on my phone. I'm writing this book, after all. Instead, I studied the menu, even though I had already decided what I wanted.

A server dropped off a glass of water. I made small talk, just a quick mention that I was waiting for a friend before assuring him I'd hold off on ordering. Then, out of habit, I checked my phone, just in case Natalie had texted me. She hadn't. So I sent her a quick message: "I'm inside. Got us a table."

Phone down.

I exhaled. Only ten minutes had passed, but sitting alone in a restaurant without a screen to distract me felt strangely difficult. I glanced around the room. That's when I noticed three other people eating alone.

Eating lunch out alone. It had been so long, I almost forgot that people actually do this. I used to do it, years ago. Back then, it felt normal, maybe even enjoyable. But somewhere along the way, I stopped. Maybe life got busier. Maybe I got used to the constant company of my phone. Or maybe I just forgot how to sit with my own solitude.

One woman sat by the window, quietly scrolling. Another man at the bar was fully absorbed in his meal. And then, two booths in front of me, a man sat alone, facing me. For a brief moment, our eyes met. We both shared a polite, fleeting smile, the kind people exchange when they accidentally make eye contact. But that was it. No words. No acknowledgment beyond that moment.

I looked back at my menu. Again. By the time I glanced up, he was already paying his check. And just like that, the opportunity was gone.

I had the chance to say something. A simple "How's your meal?" or "Is this your first time here?" would have been enough. But I hesitated, unsure of what to say, unsure if he'd even want to talk. And in that hesitation, the moment slipped away.

It's not that I was afraid. I wasn't overthinking, and I wasn't anxious. Those are all things we've covered earlier in this book.

No, this was something different.

This was just the raw reality of making the first move. The awkwardness of not knowing how. The discomfort of stepping into the unknown. And yet, what if I had?

It wasn't a bad day. But it was a missed moment. And those are the ones that remind me just how much courage it can take to simply say hello.

The Fear of the First Move

We've already explored the common barriers to starting a conversation: fear of rejection, social anxiety, and overthinking. By now, you know that most of these fears exist more in our heads than in reality. Social psychology research shows that people actually appreciate friendly interactions far more than we assume. Striking up a conversation isn't nearly as risky as it feels.

But even with this knowledge, there's still that hesitation, that tiny voice whispering, *What if I'm bothering them? What if I come off as weird?*

You don't need to be a walking TED Talk.
A smile and a "hey" will do just fine.

Carla and Jake's Story

Carla and Jake worked in the same shopping mall, their stores just a few doors apart. Every day, they passed each other in the food court or on their way to clock in. They weren't exactly strangers; they'd exchanged nods, maybe a quick "Hey" in passing, but that was it.

Carla wanted to introduce herself properly, maybe joke about how they were practically coworkers. But what if he didn't remember her? What if he thought she was being too much?

Jake, on the other hand, had the exact same thought.

She probably doesn't know who I am. What if I say hi, and she stares at me like I'm some random guy?

So day after day, they stayed in their separate bubbles, waiting for some invisible signal that it was safe to talk.

Then, one afternoon, fate (or maybe just caffeine cravings) intervened. They ended up in line together at the mall coffee shop.

Carla glanced over. Their eyes met. Okay, she thought. Just say something. She hesitated, debating whether to say something or just wait until the moment passed like every other day. But today, something nudged her.

"Hey, I feel like I see you every day but don't actually know your name," she blurted out, half-laughing to cover her nerves.

Jake's face lit up in relief. "Right? I was just thinking the same thing! I'm Jake."

And just like that, the invisible wall crumbled.

Conversations Are Opportunities, Not Auditions

What changed? Nothing, except one person decided to stop seeing conversation as a performance to be judged and started seeing it as an opportunity to connect.

Carla didn't need the perfect opening line. She didn't need to be witty, interesting, or cool. She just needed to acknowledge reality: Hey, I see you. Let's talk.

If you've ever hesitated to start a conversation because you weren't sure how it would be received, here's something to remember:

Most people are just as uncertain as you are. They're waiting for permission, a cue, a tiny nudge that says, It's okay to talk. And more often than not, they'll welcome the chance.

So the next time you find yourself hesitating, remind yourself: This isn't a test. There's nothing to win or lose. It's just a moment. A small, human opportunity to turn a nod into a hello, and maybe even something more.

The Power of the First Impression

First impressions happen fast. Studies suggest that people form an opinion about you within seconds of meeting you, sometimes before you've even spoken. While that might sound intimidating, it's actually a good thing. It means that small, intentional shifts in how you present yourself can make you seem more approachable, confident, and interesting before you even open your mouth.

We covered body language in depth back in Chapter 9, so you already know that how you carry yourself, your posture, facial expressions, and gestures play a huge role in how people perceive you. But beyond posture and eye contact, there's something equally powerful at play when it comes to making the first move: energy and curiosity.

The Unexpected Friendship

Margaret had been eating lunch at the same deli for months. Every Thursday, same time, same corner table. And every Thursday, she'd see the same older man sitting a few tables away, reading a newspaper.

She'd noticed small things about him over time: how he always ordered soup, how he underlined certain passages in the paper, how he nodded at familiar faces but never seemed to start a conversation himself.

One afternoon, as she stood near the register waiting for her coffee, the opportunity was there. The moment she could either say something or just go back to her usual table.

She hesitated. What if he doesn't want to talk? What if he thinks I'm being nosy?

But instead of seeing it as a risk, she reframed it as a simple chance to connect.

She glanced at the newspaper in his hands and said, "That must be a good read. I see you marking things every week."

The man looked up, startled for a moment, then smiled. "It's a habit. I used to teach history, and I can't seem to break the habit of grading things."

Margaret laughed. "So you're still giving the news a passing or failing grade?"

He chuckled. "Most days, it's not doing so well."

And just like that, a friendship began.

How Curiosity Makes You Instantly More Interesting

Margaret didn't walk into that café thinking, I need to impress someone today. She simply noticed something and asked about it.

That's the magic of curiosity. It's an effortless way to be engaging. You don't need to have fascinating stories, clever jokes, or dazzling charisma. You just need to take a genuine interest in the person you're talking to.

Want to make a great first impression? Instead of worrying about how you look to others, focus on how you make them feel.

- **Make eye contact and smile** – It's the easiest way to show warmth.
- **Ask a casual question** – "What's that book you're reading?" is a better icebreaker than "What do you do for work?"
- **Mirror their energy** – If they seem chatty, match their enthusiasm. If they're more reserved, keep it easygoing.

Most people aren't judging you as harshly as you think. In fact, they're often just waiting for someone to open the door to a conversation. A single moment of curiosity can be the difference between a missed connection and a lasting one.

When in Doubt, Just C.H.A.T.
Compliment. Help. Ask. Tie It to the Moment.

You don't need the perfect words to start a conversation, just the willingness to open a door. When in doubt, you can always C.H.A.T. It's a simple way to remember four types of universal icebreakers that work in nearly any situation.

Next time you're in a class, coffee shop, bookstore, gym, dog park, grocery store, restaurant, party, waiting room, or even just in line at the grocery store or on a train, try using these to spark up a conversation. They're great for breaking the ice and making connections wherever you are. Enjoy!

C = Compliment

A simple, **genuine compliment** is one of the easiest ways to start a conversation. While we might feel awkward giving compliments, the truth is people actually appreciate them more than we think.

The trick is to be specific and focus on something the other person has chosen, like their clothing, accessories, or skills. A friendly and thoughtful compliment shows genuine warmth and interest, making the interaction feel more natural and pleasant.

Why it works: Compliments have a magical way of breaking down barriers and making people feel special without being pushy. When someone receives a kind word, it often brings a smile to their face and brightens their day. It's all about noticing the little things.

Start with warmth. A small, sincere compliment is often the fastest way to create ease.

- "That's a great jacket! That color looks great on you." (In a classroom)
- "I love your tattoo! Is there a story behind it?" (In line at a grocery store)
- "These are nice! You have such a great eye, and your photos turned out amazing."
  (At a community event)
- "Your dog is so well-trained! How long did it take to teach that trick?"
  (At a dog park)

H = Help or Humor

People really enjoy being helpful! When you ask someone for a small favor or their opinion, it's a fantastic way to kick off a conversation and make them feel appreciated. Adding a touch of humor can also work wonders. If the vibe is right, a lighthearted comment can really help everyone feel more relaxed and comfortable.

Why it works: Shared humanity builds trust. Being kind or relatable helps people feel safe, not just heard.

Ask for help with something small: information, their opinion.

- "I'm terrible at choosing books—have you read this one before?" (At a bookstore)
- "Hey, do you know if this train stops near Central Park?" (On public transportation)

- "I'm new to this gym—do you know if there's a sign-up for this class?" (At a fitness center)
- "I can never remember—do you tip at a coffee bar or just at the table?" (At a café)

Use gentle, self-aware **humor** to disarm tension.

- "You'd think picking a sauce wouldn't be this stressful." (At a grocery store)
- "I swear, they make these waiting rooms extra cold to keep us awake." (At a doctor's office)
- "Do you think if we both stare at the menu long enough, we'll magically know what to order?" (At a restaurant)
- "I think I just did five minutes of cardio looking for the shortest checkout line." (At a store)

A = Ask Something Personal (But Light)

People love to talk about things they're interested in. If you notice something unique about them—a book they're reading, a cool accessory, or an activity they're doing—commenting on it can be a great way to start a conversation.

Why it works: Questions show you're interested, not just interesting. They shift the focus from small talk to shared meaning.

Ask something real, but not too deep, about the other person's experience.

- "That book looks interesting. Have you read other books by that author?" (At a bookstore)
- "I saw you sketching earlier. Are you an artist?" (At a park)

- "That's a cool keychain. Is there a story behind it?" (In class)
- "Your playlist sounds awesome! What song was that?" (At the gym)

T= Tie the Moment

Notice something happening right now, around you, between you, or in the room. The environment, common interests, or situations make for easy conversation starters.

Why it works: You don't need a script. You just need the moment. It makes conversation feel organic and grounded in shared space.

When you're in the same environment as someone, you already have something in common, and that shared experience makes for an easy conversation starter.

- "That was a long speech. What did you think?" (At a wedding or work event)
- "I didn't expect that ending! Did you see that twist coming?" (After a movie or lecture)
- "Have you ever taken a class with this professor before? I hear he gives impossible exams." (College classroom)
- "This is my first time at this book club. Have you been coming long?" (At a meetup or club meeting)

If you notice that you share an interest, hobby, or passion with someone else, bringing it up is an easy way to start a conversation.

- "Are you a regular at this trivia night? You look like you know what you're doing." (At a game night)

- "Is that a camera lens tattoo? Are you a photographer?" (Noticing someone's tattoo or accessory)
- "I can never decide. What's your go-to drink here?" (At a coffee shop)

When in doubt, talk about what's happening around you. Situational openers feel effortless because they don't require any special knowledge or wit; just simple awareness.

- "Wow, this line is taking forever. Do they always take this long?" (At a bakery)
- "I didn't expect this place to be so packed on a Tuesday. Have you been here before?" (At a restaurant)
- "They're playing great music here. Do you know this band?" (At a coffee shop)
- "This professor talks so fast! Do you actually get all the notes down?" (In class)

You don't have to be clever. You don't have to be polished. Just start somewhere warm. Somewhere kind.

When in doubt—C.H.A.T.

Keeping the Conversation Flowing

So you've broken the ice. You started the conversation, and they responded positively. Now what? This is where a lot of people freeze up. They think, *What if I run out of things to say? What if there's an awkward silence?* The good news? Keeping a conversation going is way easier than people think.

> The secret isn't about coming up with
> interesting things to say.
> It's about making the other person feel interesting.

The Follow-Up Formula

A conversation should feel like tossing a ball back and forth, not like you're carrying all the weight of keeping it going. The easiest way to do this?

> The Follow-Up Formula:
> Listen → Relate → Ask.

This formula keeps the conversation moving without feeling forced.

1. **Listen** → Pay close attention to what they're saying. Don't just wait for your turn to talk; really hear them.
2. **Relate** → Share something that connects to what they said. It doesn't have to be a long story. Just a quick way to keep the conversation natural.
3. **Ask** → Keep the momentum going by asking a follow-up question.

Examples of the Follow-Up Formula in Action

Them: "I just got back from Italy. It was amazing."

You: "That's incredible! I went there a few years ago and fell in love with the food. What was your favorite part of the trip?"

Them: "I love running. It helps me clear my mind."

You: "I'm the same way with long walks. Do you run marathons or just for fun?"

The First Date That Almost Flopped

Charlie was starting to look forward to first dates. But he worried too much about what to say and often ended up rambling to fill awkward silences.

So when he met Leah at a coffee shop for their first date, he decided to try something different: He focused on asking good questions and really listening.

At first, Leah was a little reserved, but when she mentioned she loved rock climbing, Charlie followed the formula:

Listen → She talked about how she started climbing in college.

Relate → He admitted he had tried once but got stuck halfway up the wall.

Ask → "How long did it take you to get good at it?"

That simple question opened the door for a deeper conversation. Leah started sharing stories about her favorite climbs, her dream of visiting Yosemite, and how she convinced her little sister to try it.

By the end of the date, Leah felt like she had a great time, not because Charlie had said anything brilliant, but because he had made her feel interesting.

Matching Conversation Depth and Energy

One of the easiest ways to keep a conversation engaging is to read the room and adjust accordingly.

- If someone is sharing something personal, don't stay surface-level. If they open up about their love of writing, instead of just saying "That's cool!", ask about what they like to write or their dream project.
- If they keep things light, follow their lead. Not every conversation has to be deep. If they're joking around about their bad luck in fantasy football, jumping into a heavy topic might feel out of place.
- Gauge how much they want to engage. If they're giving one-word answers and checking their phone, it might not be the best moment for a long chat. But if they're making eye contact, asking you questions back, and expanding on their thoughts, they're likely enjoying the conversation.

The Friendly Neighbor

Eric was out for a walk when he passed his neighbor, Mr. Patel, watering his garden. They exchanged waves, and Eric casually said, "Your tomatoes are looking great!" Mr. Patel smiled. "Thanks! This heat has been brutal, though. I have to water them twice a day."

Now, **Eric had a choice.** He could just nod and keep walking, or he could match the conversation depth. Instead of just replying "Yeah, it's been hot," he showed interest and engaged further: "I can imagine! Have you been growing vegetables for a long time?"

That small shift turned a passing hello into a friendly chat about gardening, family recipes, and their neighborhood, without forcing anything unnatural.

Sometimes, kindness sounds like curiosity. And sometimes, connection grows in two minutes between tomato plants.

The Power of Small Self-Disclosures

People are more likely to open up when you open up a little first. The key is small self-disclosures, little personal details that show you're engaged without dominating the conversation.

Example 1

    Them: "I love baking."

    You: "That's awesome! I've always wanted to get better at baking, but I burn cookies like it's my superpower. What's your favorite thing to bake?"

Example 2

    Them: "I just moved here a few months ago."

    You: "That's exciting! I remember when I first moved, I got lost every time I drove somewhere new. How are you liking it so far?"

These little personal touches make the conversation feel like a two-way street rather than an interview.

The Classmates Who Became Friends

Carmen and Amy sat next to each other in a college lecture hall every week but never really talked. One day, before class started, Amy sighed and muttered, "I don't think I'm ever going to understand this professor."

Instead of just agreeing, Carmen added, "Right? I feel like I'm in a completely different language class. I started watching YouTube videos just to keep up."

Amy laughed. "Wait, you found a good YouTube tutor? Send me the link. I need all the help I can get."

That tiny moment of self-disclosure shifted their dynamic from two strangers sitting next to each other to people who could relate and connect.

Creating Conversations People Enjoy

At this point, you've started a conversation. You've broken the ice, found some common ground, and things are moving along. But now comes the bigger challenge: keeping it going in a way that feels natural and engaging.

Many people think the key to a great conversation is being interesting. But the truth is, great conversations feel effortless, not because one person is fascinating, but because both people feel included and engaged.

That's the real secret to being someone people love talking to: make the conversation enjoyable for both of you.

Here's how to do that without forcing it.

1. Keep the Balance Between Talking and Listening

Ever been in a conversation where one person talks endlessly about themselves while you just nod and smile? Or, on the flip side, where someone asks a million questions but never shares anything about themselves?

Both of these can make a conversation feel one-sided.

A good rule of thumb: Treat conversations like a friendly game of ping-pong. The ball should go back and forth, with each person taking turns adding something new to the discussion.

- Instead of just asking questions, share small personal stories too.
- Instead of just talking about yourself, ask the other person about their experience.

Example of Balance in Conversation

Them: "I went hiking last weekend. It was brutal but fun."

You: "I love hiking too! I did a really tough trail last summer. Where did you go?"

You acknowledged their experience, shared something about yourself, and invited them to continue talking. This feels natural, rather than like an interview or a monologue.

2. Know When to Share a Quick Story

Weaving in small, relevant stories makes a conversation more engaging, but timing is everything.

The best stories:

- Are short and to the point (not a five-minute saga).
- Connect naturally to the topic at hand.
- Invite a response (leaving room for the other person to add their thoughts).

Example of a Well-Timed Story

If someone mentions their childhood pet:

Wrong Approach: "Oh, that reminds me! I had a dog named Buddy, and he was a rescue, and when I first got him, he was so scared, but over time he warmed up, and then one time he ran away, and we searched for hours, and then he came back covered in mud, and it was crazy because... (five minutes later)... Anyway, so yeah, dogs are great."

Better Approach: "I had a dog growing up, too! He was a rescue and was super timid at first, but once he got comfortable, he had the funniest personality. What kind of pet did you have?"

This keeps the story concise, engaging, and open-ended, rather than hijacking the conversation.

3. Use Humor and Playfulness Naturally

You don't need to be a comedian to make a conversation fun. But a little lightheartedness can go a long way in making interactions feel comfortable.

Humor works best when:
- It's situational. (Commenting on something happening in the moment)
- It's self-aware. (Playfully making fun of yourself can make people feel at ease.)
- It's inclusive. (Avoid humor that makes the other person uncomfortable.)

Making Friends on Trivia Night

At a trivia night, Cory got paired with a stranger, Olivia. At first, their team was quiet, just throwing out answers. But after a few rounds, Cory leaned over and said,

"Alright, I have a theory: every trivia team has 'the history buff' and 'the one who's weirdly good at knowing all the state capitals. Which one are you?"

Olivia laughed. "Neither. But if there's a round on bad 2000s pop music, I'll carry us."

That playful remark shifted the mood, and soon they were swapping stories about their most embarrassing karaoke performances. The night went from a quiet game to an actual conversation, and they ended up meeting up for trivia every week after.

Why it worked: Cory kept it light and inclusive. It gave Olivia an easy way to respond (without putting her on the spot). It set the tone for a relaxed, fun conversation.

A great conversation isn't about impressing someone. It's about making the interaction feel effortless and enjoyable.

Having friendly conversations is all about making others feel really heard, valued, and engaged! When you create a relaxed vibe and enjoy a nice back-and-forth, you leave a good impression—no need to be the most fascinating person around. Conversation is all about balance. Make sure to listen closely, share your thoughts naturally, and let the chat flow easily. Remember, it's not about being the best at talking, but about being someone others enjoy chatting with!

When you take the pressure off yourself and focus on connection over performance, conversations won't just feel easier—they'll become something you and the other person genuinely enjoy.

Every conversation begins with a risk, the risk of being ignored, misunderstood, or dismissed. But it also carries a quiet promise: the possibility of connection, understanding, and even unexpected joy. When you're brave enough to say hello first, you open the door not just to small talk but to something much bigger. Something human. Something real.

Whether it's a two-minute chat with a stranger or a deeper talk with someone new, every interaction helps you get better.

You never know, a single conversation could change everything.

What This Means: Starting a conversation is about being present, curious, and willing to reach out. Saying hello first isn't small; it's a brave act of invitation. You don't need the perfect words. You just need to go first.

Why It Matters: In a world where so many people feel unseen or overlooked, your willingness to initiate—even with a simple greeting—can change everything. People don't remember clever lines. They remember how it felt to be noticed, welcomed, and drawn into something real. Connection begins where fear ends.

What Comes Next: The next time you feel the urge to speak to someone, honor it. Don't overthink it. Just start. A smile. A question. A comment about the moment you're both in. Let go of the pressure to be interesting and focus on being open. You never know who's waiting for someone to go first.

Want more friends?
Stop trying to be interesting.
Start being interested.
That simple shift can build
more real connections in weeks
than most manage in years.

Chapter 12

Navigating Friendship: Where to Meet, How to Connect

"Friendship is born at that moment when one person says to another: 'What! You too? I thought I was the only one."
– C.S. Lewis

Maybe it hits you at the end of a long day. You got good news, an award at school, a promotion at work, even a funny text from your kid, and you instinctively reach for your phone.... but pause. **Who do you tell? Who actually knows what this means to you?**

Or maybe it's something quieter. You scroll social media, half hoping for a message or a sign that someone's thinking of you.

You're not the only one. Millions of people—teens trying to fit in, college students figuring out their next steps, young adults launching into the world, parents holding everything together, retirees stepping into new chapters—are quietly wondering the same thing:

Where do I even begin?

It's not that anything's wrong with you. It's just that our world isn't set up for connection the way it once was. With constant distractions, packed schedules, and the pull of comfort zones, it's no wonder real friendship feels harder to reach.

But here's the truth: Friendships don't just happen.

They grow with intention, time, and just a little courage to stretch beyond what feels safe. This chapter will help you notice where connection lives and how to move toward it.

THE FRIENDSHIP COMPASS
A New Way to Navigate Connection

Making new friends as an adult isn't about luck—it's about noticing the moments where connection is possible.

Think of friendship as less of a search and more of a compass—a way to navigate toward warmth, safety, and real belonging.

Each point of the compass helps us find our way, not just socially, but also emotionally and physiologically.

Connection is:
Emotional. Physical. Relational. Rhythmic.

As you learned earlier, our bodies are wired for interpersonal synchrony, an almost invisible dance where emotions, energy, and heartbeats start to align.

This compass helps us understand how and where that rhythm can start to take shape.

⊘ COMPASS POINT	WHAT IT LOOKS LIKE
NORTH	Proximity + Repetition
EAST	Shared Experiences
SOUTH	Balance and Reciprocity
WEST	Authentic Energy

⊘ NORTH: Proximity + Repetition

Safety through familiarity. Repeated exposure in low-pressure spaces creates emotional ease and trust.

We're more likely to bond with the people we see often. The classmate. The neighbor. The person in the same yoga class every Tuesday.

This is more than convenience, it's biology. The brain rewards familiarity. The more we see someone in a safe, positive space, the more trust grows. Mirror neurons fire. We feel more relaxed. Dopamine rises. And just like that, someone goes from stranger to "Oh hey, it's you again."

Trust doesn't happen all at once.
It happens every time you return.

🧭 EAST: Shared Moments and Experiences

Connection grows when we do things side-by-side: whether it's hiking, laughing, stretching, or even grieving.

In these brief moments, something really cool happens: we start to sync up with each other. Our nervous systems, which are pretty complex, begin to vibe together. Without even realizing it, we copy each other's body language, match our breathing, and echo the sounds of our voices. This is empathy in action, a quiet dance of connection. It's how we show we understand each other and are really present, all without saying a word. It creates a space where we truly feel noticed and understood.

> *Want to feel close to someone? Move with them.*
> *Cook with them. Walk with them.*
> *Laugh at the same thing.*
> *That's where connection lives.*

🧭 SOUTH: Balance and Reciprocity

The best friendships feel mutual. You don't always give the same things at the same time, but you feel the give and take. There's curiosity in both directions. There's care.

Earlier in the book, we explored how our emotional brains pay attention to times when our energy feels lopsided.

Too much one-way effort? It feels unsafe.

Too little vulnerability? It feels shallow.

> *True friendship isn't a transaction. It's a rhythm.*
> *And you both help keep the beat.*

⊘ WEST: Authentic Energy

You don't have to be the funniest, smartest, or most outgoing person in the room to make a real connection. What matters most is being genuine, showing up as your true self.

People don't connect to a performance or a show; they connect to presence. When your words, your body language, and the energy you give off all line up and tell the same story, something powerful happens. People start to trust you. They let their guard down. And suddenly, they feel safe enough to be themselves too.

Friendship begins where performance ends.
The real you is enough.

This compass won't give you exact coordinates. But it can help you notice when you're moving in the right direction, toward real connection, emotional resonance, and the kind of friendships that hold up in real life. And here's something important to remember: Friendships don't form overnight.

Research suggests it takes about
50 hours to move from acquaintance to casual friend, and
over 200 hours to build a truly close bond.

That might sound like a lot. But those hours aren't earned in dramatic heart-to-hearts.

They're built in small, ordinary ways: showing up. Following through. Laughing over something dumb. Being seen, even briefly, and being willing to come back again.

Real friendship is built slowly.
And that's part of what makes it strong.

To bring these ideas to life, we'll follow six people in very different life stages, each navigating what it means to start over, reach out, or reconnect.

Julia is 18 and just started at Emory University, a well-known university in Atlanta. It's October, and she feels like everyone else has already found their group. Old friends aren't replying like they used to, and she's not sure how to join in when she hears people making Halloween plans.

Cory is 20, a business major at Emory, starting over after a breakup shattered his old friend group. Between classes, work, and volunteering, he's discovering that friendships take time to rebuild and come with less pressure.

Zoe is 24 and recently moved to Atlanta for her first job out of college. She works remotely, lives alone, and is slowly realizing that building adult friendships requires more courage than she expected.

Nate is 39, a single father of two, recently divorced. Between juggling co-parenting and healing from heartache, he's not sure how to rebuild his social life or if there's room for him in anyone else's.

Priya is 55, a working mom with teenagers and aging parents. She's built a life around caring for others, but often feels like her friendships have slipped into the background.

Diane is 72, newly retired, and adjusting to life in a new town to be closer to her grandchildren. She's warm and quietly observant, but starting over in her seventies has left her feeling invisible.

We'll begin with two students from Emory University in Atlanta, because college is one of the most common and often most vulnerable times to build friendships from scratch.

Julia: Finding Her Footing

Julia is 18 and just a few weeks into her first semester as a psychology major at Emory University. The blur of welcome events has faded, and the campus is settling into its routines. But Julia hasn't found her people yet.

Her group project teammates are nice, and her roommate is fine, but most days, she eats alone in the dining hall. As October arrives, so do the Halloween plans. She hears classmates making group plans between lectures, excited about haunted houses and themed parties. Julia doesn't know how to join the conversation, let alone the event.

She texts her high school friends for comfort, but they're busy with new circles of their own. It feels like everyone else has already found their friends.

One Thursday after class, she hesitates at her desk while others file out. A voice beside her says, "That midterm review went by fast, huh?"

It's Cory, a junior who sits a few rows up. They strike up a conversation, first about class, then about their shared love of true crime podcasts.

Before leaving, Cory says, "There's a volunteer event this weekend, Emory Cares. I'll be there if you're free."

Julia almost says no. But instead, she says, "Maybe I'll check it out."

She shows up. No huge transformation. Just gloves, sorting boxes, casual chats. But it's the first time in weeks she doesn't feel invisible.

Compass Points:

🧭 **Repetition** – Same psych class becomes a familiar rhythm

🧭 **Shared Experience** – Volunteering side-by-side lowers the pressure

🧭 **Authentic Energy** – Julia didn't need to perform. She just showed up

Cory: Starting Over, Again

At 20, Cory thought he had it figured out. A business major in his junior year at Emory, he'd built a strong social life: weekend hikes, late-night group chats, study sessions that turned into spontaneous pizza nights.

Then the breakup happened, not just the end of a relationship but also the loss of a whole friend circle. Some friends chose sides, and others quietly disappeared. It wasn't his first reset. Cory had transferred to Emory sophomore year and remembered how it felt to start over. That's what saved him.

He worked more hours at his campus job and started volunteering on Saturdays. Not because he was chasing friendship, but because he knew showing up mattered. Movement made space for connection.

In psych class, he noticed a quiet freshman, Julia, lingering after the lecture. She looked like someone searching for a place to land. He struck up a simple conversation and invited her to the volunteer event. He didn't overthink it. He just made room.

He still wasn't sure what his new circle would look like. But this time, he wasn't trying to rebuild the old one. He was letting something new form slowly.

Compass Points:

- **Shared Experience** – Serving side-by-side allowed casual connection
- **Repetition** – Showing up again gave him momentum
- **Authentic Energy** – Cory didn't force anything. He just showed up, open

Zoe: Showing Up in a New City

Zoe had been in Atlanta for almost four months, and she was starting to feel like a ghost.

She'd moved for a remote job at a tech company, fresh start, her own place, no roommates. But the silence between Slack messages stretched longer than she'd expected. Most days, her only in-person interactions were with the barista downstairs.

One Tuesday, she signed up for a beginner yoga class at a studio near her apartment in Midtown. She didn't own a mat yet, but she reminded herself this wasn't really about yoga. It was about not disappearing.

By the third week, she began to notice familiar faces, especially the woman who quietly took the mat next to hers again. Zoe recognized her from week one. They exchanged a smile. Nothing dramatic. Just something soft and human.

In week five, that woman, Priya, laughed when Zoe nearly fell during a balance pose. "That's what I get for trying to be graceful," Zoe said.

Priya replied, "I figure if I'm going to fall, I might as well do it confidently."

They both smiled, and Zoe realized: this was the first time in weeks she felt like herself again.

Compass Points:

⊘ **Proximity + Repetition** – Same studio, same mat spot

⊘ **Authentic Energy** – Awkwardness embraced, not hidden

⊘ **Shared Experience** – Laughing through a wobbly pose becomes the beginning of familiarity

Nate: Starting Over

Nate hadn't planned to be parenting solo at 39. But life had rearranged itself quickly: divorce, shared custody, a quieter house on the weekends.

He hadn't made new friends in years. Most of his energy went into his kids, his job, and avoiding awkward small talk at school events.

His mom, Diane, had recently moved nearby and suggested he find a hobby that didn't involve snacks or screen time.

"You used to love hiking," she reminded him.

He signed up for a local trail group. Low-key, Saturday mornings, no pressure. The first time, he almost didn't go. But once he started walking, breathing, and listening to the group's easy chatter, something settled.

He didn't stay for coffee afterward. Not the first time.

But he did go back.

A guy from the group asked, "Hey, you're Nate, right?"

That was all it took.

Compass Points:

🧭 **Shared Experience** – Hiking gives space to connect without forced eye contact

🧭 **Repetition** – Showing up more than once helps him become a known presence

🧭 **Authentic Energy** – He doesn't fake confidence; he just shows up as he is

Priya: Reconnecting with Herself

Priya is 55, a working mom balancing two teenagers, a demanding job, and aging parents. She spends most of her social energy caregiving, whether at work, at home, or with her extended family.

Her friendships have become more about quick texts and shared logistics than actual connection. She misses deeper conversations but often feels too drained to reach out.

One Saturday, she signs up for a local volunteer day through her company. She spends the morning organizing supplies next to a college student named Cory. Their conversation is easy, with no expectations.

On the drive home, she realizes it's the first time in months she felt like herself. Not just someone helping others, but someone with others.

Compass Points:

- **Shared Experience** – Volunteering created a low-pressure connection
- **Proximity** – Being side-by-side opened space for casual talk
- **Authentic Energy** – Priya didn't plan it; she just allowed herself to be present

Diane: Making Space for New Beginnings

Diane is 72, newly retired, and recently moved to Atlanta to be closer to her grandchildren. Her days are slower now, filled with routines and quiet.

She's warm, thoughtful, and curious. But starting over in her seventies feels disorienting. The neighborhood feels younger. She misses being known.

After months of settling in, she signs up for a local library book club. She doesn't say much at the first meeting, but someone remembers her name the second time. It surprises her how much that matters.

She begins attending more regularly, not because she's made best friends, but because she's carving out space for them to exist.

Compass Points:
- **Repetition** – Attending consistently helped her feel remembered
- **Shared Experience** – A common topic made small talk easier
- **Authentic Energy** – Diane stayed quiet but open

It's not about being wildly social.
It's about letting your life become just visible enough
that someone else can find you there.

The Village Still Matters

There's a reason people say "it takes a village." Because the truth is, friendship doesn't always arrive through big, dramatic moments. Sometimes it builds in layers. Quietly. Over time.

One surprising lesson from happiness research is that our daily happiness isn't only affected by our closest relationships. It is also shaped by the familiar faces we see regularly.

We don't always call these people friends. But they hold part of our lives. And that matters.

The woman who remembers your coffee order. The pharmacist who asks how your child is feeling. The guy who always walks his dog at the same time you do. The neighbor who waves from the porch and remembers your name. And the dry cleaner who asks how your daughter's school is going.

These aren't deep conversations. They're something even more rare these days: reliable, low-pressure warmth. Chapter 4 explored this idea—the power of small connections to lift our mood and remind us we're part of something bigger. But during the pandemic, many of those rhythms disappeared.

The sushi restaurant owner, the librarian, the gym front-desk worker—they became names in emails or faces behind masks, if we saw them at all.

Now, we're relearning how to reconnect in these everyday spaces.

For many of us, community is being rebuilt not in sweeping gestures but in tiny hellos, small talk that becomes ritual, and strangers who start to feel familiar again.

Where to Meet New People

There's no single right place to make new friends. But there are places where connection grows best—where the compass points overlap. You don't need to go somewhere loud or wildly social. You just need to go somewhere where people show up more than once, where shared experience is possible, and where your presence can slowly become familiar.

Dorm Lounge (Julia)

 *Compass Point: Proximity + Repetition*

Julia noticed the same few people in her dorm's common room every week, but always assumed they already had their friend groups. One evening, instead of putting in earbuds, she stayed on the couch and commented on someone's Halloween decorations. Taking that small risk to speak up started a real conversation.

Community Tip: Look for repeated faces in low-pressure places (lounges, laundry rooms, shared kitchens). Small comments open big doors.

Campus Volunteer Event (Cory)

Compass Point: Shared Experience + Authentic Energy

After losing his friend group, Cory didn't want to "start over" with small talk. He signed up for a volunteer event at his university with no expectations, just wanting to do something useful. Helping others side by side gave space for a natural connection.

Community Tip: Join something that matters to you. Friendships formed around shared purpose often feel more meaningful and less forced.

Yoga (Zoe)

Compass Point: Proximity + Repetition

Zoe's neighborhood yoga studio wasn't about perfect form; it was about being seen. Each week, she showed up. Each week, someone noticed.

Community Tip: Don't leave immediately after class. Linger five extra minutes.

> Repetition + one small exchange =
> the beginning of something.

Local Hiking Meetup (Nate)

Compass Point: Shared Experience

Nate didn't want a deep talk. What he really needed was a trail, a water bottle, and someone who noticed when he returned again.

Community Tip: Look for activity-based meetups. Movement creates comfort. Connection often begins side by side before it turns face-to-face.

Bookstore or Library Volunteering (Diane)

Compass Point: Reciprocity + Repetition

Diane wasn't looking for attention. She was searching for rhythm and found it in returning books, saying hello again, and small conversations that added up to something real.

Community Tip: Serving others can be the softest way to step into community, especially when you feel invisible.

Recurring Interest-Based Group (Priya)

Compass Point: Shared Experience + Authentic Energy

Priya didn't need to talk about her life right away. She just needed to be somewhere her full self was welcome, with no roles and no pressure. The weekly yoga class let her body relax before her heart followed.

Community Tip: Don't wait for time to "open up." Claim it one consistent hour at a time.

Other Places Where Friendships Often Begin

SETTING	WHY IT WORKS
Local coffee shops	Familiar faces + low-stakes small talk builds rhythm
Dog parks	Repetition, shared purpose, low-pressure entry points
Religious or spiritual communities	Repetition, shared values, multigenerational mix
Support groups / wellness classes	Authenticity + shared vulnerability from the start
Community education / adult learning	Shared focus, consistency, personal growth setting
Farmers markets / co-ops	Neighborhood rhythm, small interactions, eye contact
School events / parent volunteering	Built-in repetition, shared goals, quick bonds
Classes or creative hobbies	Built-in structure + shared focus lowers pressure to "perform" socially; repeated exposure allows connection to grow naturally
Local hiking or walking groups	Side-by-side movement lowers pressure, builds familiarity

You don't need to be a great artist or a confident extrovert. Just someone willing to be a beginner at something fun, and maybe at friendship too.

You don't need to meet everyone. You just need to start showing up where connections can grow. And sometimes, it's not about where you go; it's about how you go.

In the next section, we'll look at some common friendship roadblocks and what to do when you hit them.

Common Pitfalls on the Path to Friendship

Even when we mean well, we all have those times when we get stuck! Let's take a look at four relatable moments for a little insight into the ups and downs we all face.

Julia: Assuming Everyone Else Has It Figured Out

Julia walked through campus, surrounded by people laughing and talking in tight friend groups. Everyone seemed to belong somewhere already. She sat in the dining hall scrolling through old group chats from high school, but replies were slow now because everyone was busy with their "new" lives.

She overheard girls in class making Halloween plans and wished she knew how to join in. But it felt too late, like the friend doors had already closed.

Lesson: Most people are still figuring it out too. Don't believe the highlight reel. Look for one person, one moment, and start there.

Cory: Comparing This Year to Last Year

Cory didn't expect to be starting over. He already knew the rhythms of campus life. But after a rough breakup, the group he once called "his people" faded fast. Study sessions stopped. Weekend plans disappeared.

At first, it stung. Then he signed up to volunteer again, reconnected with classmates, and started building a new circle, not the same but still real.

Lesson: Starting over doesn't mean you failed. It means you're growing. Comparison keeps you stuck in the past; connection pulls you forward.

Zoe: Waiting to Be Invited

Zoe kept showing up to yoga, smiling, taking the same spot by the window. But deep down, she still hoped someone would talk to her first. Maybe they'd compliment her leggings or ask where she got her mat (Target clearance rack, obviously).

After week five with no meaningful conversation, she started wondering: Is there such a thing as friendship repellent, and am I wearing it? The truth? Everyone else was wondering the same thing. Sometimes, the difference between connection and disconnection is one person willing to go first.

Lesson: Don't wait for an invitation. You might be the invitation someone else is waiting for.

Nate: Over-Investing Too Soon

After one great hike, Nate thought he might've found his "friend soulmate." They'd both groaned about blisters, had matching kid snacks in their backpacks, and even liked the same sports team. This is it, he thought. My adult friendship breakthrough.

So he texted. And followed up. And maybe... followed up again. Crickets. Now, every time his phone buzzed, it felt like emotional Russian roulette.

Lesson: Not every friendly person is meant to become a friend. Keep showing up, but hold people loosely at first.

Priya: Good Intentions, No Follow-Through

Priya had mastered the art of friendly flakiness. She meant it every time she said, "Let's grab coffee soon!" But between work, laundry, and the eternal mystery of what's for dinner, "soon" kept turning into "someday" and then... silence.

She wasn't avoiding people. She was just tired. Chronically. Perpetually. Systemically.

Eventually, she realized the guilt was worse than the risk of getting it wrong.

Lesson: Start small. Friendship doesn't have to be fully planned to begin. A quick text. A shared walk. Just one step forward.

Diane: Assuming It's Too Late

Diane had officially decided that everyone in town already had their lifelong friend groups established sometime around 1993. So she stayed quiet, shelving books at the library, watching the same people pass by with what looked like effortless connection.

Then someone turned to her and said, "You're new, right? I'm so glad someone else is figuring this out too. I thought I was the only one."

Diane nearly cried. And then nearly laughed at how wrong she'd been.

Lesson: Most people are hoping to connect. Your presence might be the relief someone else needs.

Friendship isn't always easy. It's vulnerable. It takes effort, awkwardness, and more patience than most of us want to admit. But it also gives us something we deeply need: a place to be known. Not all at once. Not by everyone.

Just enough to remind us we're not walking through life alone.

What This Means: Friendship doesn't require a dramatic beginning. It starts in yoga classes, walking trails, and library desks. You don't need the perfect words. You need rhythm. Openness. One more hello than you gave yesterday.

Why It Matters: Because friendship isn't just social. It's essential. It steadies us. Softens our nervous systems. Reminds us we belong. The village still matters. And we need it more than ever.

What Comes Next:

- Go somewhere consistent.
- Stay five minutes longer.
- Say hello first, yes, even if it's awkward.
- Then go back again.

Don't chase best friends. Build rhythms. Be interruptible. Let people become familiar. Because sometimes, the biggest friendships begin in the smallest moments, when you show up, breathe through the awkwardness, and try again next week.

> *"Each friend represents a world in us,*
> *a world possibly not born until they arrive,*
> *and it is only by this meeting that a new world is born."*
>
> — *Anaïs Nin*

Bonus Chapter

Need a Friend? Get a Dog

"Dogs have a way of finding the people who need them, and filling an emptiness we didn't ever know we had."

– Thom Jones

Feeling lonely? You're not alone. And here's a thought: maybe the perfect solution has four legs, a wagging tail, and a heart full of love. Dogs aren't just pets—they're lifesavers. They give you a reason to step outside, show up for the day, and stay grounded in the here and now.

Think about it. You come home to someone who's always happy to see you, no judgment, no expectations. Just love. Pure, tail-wagging, unconditional love.

It's not just something we imagine. Science backs it up. Studies show that interacting with a dog releases oxytocin, the same hormone that creates feelings of love and connection with humans. But honestly? What dogs give us goes far beyond science. It's almost magical. They seem to know when we need them most, nudging us out of isolation, pulling us back into the world, and anchoring us to the present moment.

For many of us, a dog isn't just a pet. It's a lifeline.

> Need a friend? I've been there. And I can tell you this: nothing beats the kind of friend who greets you with a wagging tail and unconditional love, no matter how lonely or stuck you might feel.

This book wouldn't be complete without me sharing one of the most transformative ways I've battled loneliness: adopting a dog. Sure, I could fill this chapter with research and evidence about why having a dog is an incredible idea (and don't worry, there's some of that too). But if you've already experienced the joy of having a dog, you don't need convincing; you *know*. For those who haven't yet had that privilege, the best way I can inspire you is by sharing my personal journey and the stories of the three remarkable dogs who've shaped my life in ways I never imagined.

A Life Made Better: Three Dogs, Twenty-Five Years

Roosevelt Island is a quirky little slice of New York City, tucked between Manhattan and Queens. When my family moved there when I was 13, it was an incredible place to grow up, except for one thing: no dogs allowed. None. Zero. As a die-hard dog lover, that rule felt personal. As a little kid, I must have watched *Snoopy Come Home* a hundred times, and every time that "No Dogs Allowed" song played, I felt it deep in my soul. I dreamed of having a dog, but being a military kid meant we moved too often to make it work.

I wanted a dog who could ride in my basket, sleep at the end of my bed, and chase me through the sprinkler. I wanted a friend.

Years later, in my twenties, that dream finally came true when I adopted my first dog, Nick.

Before I ever understood the science of connection, I experienced it, curled up beside a dog who seemed to understand exactly how I felt.

Nick: My Calm Guardian

Nick was a 12-week-old chow-shepherd mix I found in an Atlanta shelter. With his thick brown fur and soulful eyes, he looked like a tiny bear cub. From day one, he had this steady, almost wise presence, like he already had life figured out.

The one thing he hadn't figured out? Being alone all day while I was at work. When he turned one, the vet told me his "accidents" weren't about potty training but stress-induced digestive issues. He was lonely. The solution? A friend.

Enter Vinny, a 12-week-old golden retriever-chow mix with boundless energy and a heart full of mischief.

Nick and Vinny became my anchors during the chaotic early years of motherhood. I didn't realize how much I'd come to rely on them until we moved to Delaware when my daughter, Stephanie, was born. Everything changed overnight. We left behind friends, family, and Georgia's warm weather for snowstorms and long weeks alone while my husband traveled for work. I was a first-time mom, adjusting to stay-at-home life, and often felt isolated. But I was never truly alone; Nick and Vinny made sure of that.

As Stephanie grew from a newborn to a toddler, our house came alive in a new way. She was fascinated by the dogs, her little giggles filling the air. Nick, patient as ever, let her grab his fur and poke his ears, his tail wagging the whole time. Mealtime became a comedy routine as he'd sit by her high chair, eyes wide, waiting for her to toss him bits of pancake or scrambled eggs.

When Stephanie learned to walk, the real fun began. She toddled after them, giggling wildly, as they played around her. Watching her grow up alongside them was magic. Nick took his role as her protector seriously, sleeping outside her door every night like a furry guardian. In the afternoons, he'd sit at the top of our cul-de-sac, quietly supervising the neighborhood kids like a watchful elder. He was my rock for nearly a decade, always there, steady and sure, reminding me that no matter how overwhelming life got, I wasn't alone.

Vinny: The Playful Best Friend

And then there was Vinny, the goofy, golden ball of energy who adored Stephanie from the start. He'd drop his toys at her feet, nudge us for attention, and engage in the best kind of chaos. One day, I caught them both teething. Vinny was gnawing his plush toy, stuffing flying like confetti, while Stephanie, in full solidarity, chewed the face off her teddy bear like it owed her money.

Where Nick was calm and stoic, Vinny was pure joy, always ready to chase the red dot from a laser pointer. With his honey-colored fur and ever-wagging tail, he made even the hardest days a little lighter. He had a sixth sense for snacks, magically appearing like a ninja in the kitchen the second a deli meat wrapper crinkled, no matter how quietly I tried to open it.

When Nick passed, Vinny grieved with us. He retreated to his "cave" behind an armoire in my bedroom, seeking comfort in his own way. But even in his sadness, he kept showing up, greeting us with gentle nudges, wagging his tail, finding little ways to remind us to smile.

As he got older, he slowed down, but his spirit never faded. When we brought home our next puppy, he patiently helped her find her place in the family. Then, at 12 years old, his body gave out. The hip pain became too much. Stephanie, just eight years old at the time, sat beside me on my bedroom floor as we said goodbye. "'Why don't dogs live as long as people?" Stephanie asked softly.

The vet's answer stayed with me: "Because they need us to take care of them."

At first, it seemed so simple. But the more I thought about it, the more I understood. Dogs come into our lives needing love and care, and in giving them that, they teach us something even greater. They show us how to love deeply, unconditionally, and without hesitation, even when we know we'll have to say goodbye.

Ginger: The Steady Witness

Nine months after losing Nick, we found ourselves back at the same Atlanta shelter. Stephanie was six years old on the day we met a Rhodesian ridgeback puppy with sleek golden fur and a distinctive ridge running down her back. She was just 17 pounds, but her giant paws hinted at the big dog she'd become. Stephanie took one look at her and declared, "She's Ginger."

Ginger grew up alongside Stephanie, photobombing birthday pictures, joining every playdate, and cementing herself as the heart of our family. She was regal but playful, always inserting herself into Stephanie's playdates, happily plopping down in the middle of blanket forts or curling up in the room during sleepovers as if she were just one of the kids.

By the time we moved to Connecticut, it was just me, Stephanie, and Ginger, starting fresh in a new place and building a new life. It was not easy finding a home to rent with a 90-pound dog. And then there was Paul, the new man in my life. From the moment they met, he and Ginger were instant pals, as if they had always known each other. She welcomed him effortlessly, sensing his kindness the way dogs do.

Paul spoiled her. Steaks became a weekly Costco staple, carefully cooked, sliced, and mixed into her food. He sang her silly little songs, and when brutal Connecticut winters hit, he bundled up to take her on walks, never once complaining about the cold.

Then, in 2020, life as we knew it came to a halt. The pandemic shutdown kept us quarantined at home, and while the world felt uncertain, one thing was undeniable: Ginger had just won the doggy lottery. Suddenly, both of us were home all day, every day, and she couldn't have been happier. She reveled in the constant company, stretching out beside our desks during Zoom calls, nudging us for midday walks, and claiming her rightful place as the true ruler of my home office. If she could've orchestrated a worldwide event to ensure we never left the house again, she absolutely would have.

For me, Ginger became a quiet, grounding presence during those years. She'd find me in the kitchen during hard days, press her head into my leg while I worked, or curl up beside me on long, anxious nights. She was always there, just quietly loving us all through it.

As the years passed, Ginger began to slow down, and we adjusted our lives to make sure she was always included. Family vacations were planned with her in mind, because leaving her behind was never an option. She became the ultimate road trip companion, happily riding along on long drives, content just to be with us. When Stephanie started college in Virginia, Ginger came along for the visits, curling up in the back as if she knew these trips were something special.

By the time she was nearly 14, her health began to fail, and we gently walked her with a dog sling, doing everything we could to keep her comfortable. In her final weeks, Paul pureed steak and chicken to make her meals easier, determined to give her every bit of love and care for as long as we could.

When it was time to say goodbye, the vet came to our home. Paul and I were both there. As I stroked Ginger's face, whispering how much we loved her, Paul rested his hand gently on her nose. She took her last breath surrounded by the people who loved her most.

That day marked the end of a journey that began with Nick and Vinny in Georgia and ended with Ginger in Connecticut. Three dogs. Twenty-five years. And a life made infinitely better because of them.

What Three Dogs Taught Me About Connection

Here's what I know: Dogs meet you exactly where you are.

Lonely? They remind you that you're never alone.

Stuck? They nudge you outside for a walk, showing you a fresh perspective.

Overwhelmed? They curl up beside you, wag their tail, and remind you to focus on the moment right in front of you.

Nick's calm grounded me.

Vinny's joy made me laugh again.

Ginger's steady spirit reminded me to keep moving forward.

They were there for the big moments, the quiet ones, and the times I didn't think I could keep going. Their shorter lives aren't a reason to avoid the love they offer. If anything, they remind us to cherish every wag, every walk, every cuddle. Because what they give us—love, companionship, and comfort—is worth every tear when it's time to say goodbye.

So if you're on the fence about adopting a dog, consider this your sign.

Go to the shelter.

Meet the dogs.

Find a friend.

Because somewhere out there, a wagging tail and a cold nose are waiting to make your life better too.

The Friend You Didn't Know You Needed

They don't care what you're wearing. They don't check your résumé. They don't interrupt you mid-sentence to tell you about their day. Dogs are, in many ways, the perfect friends.

And when loneliness hits hard or human connection feels just out of reach, sometimes it's a warm body curled beside you, tail thumping softly, that reminds you you're not alone.

For many people, a dog isn't a substitute for human friendship. It's the bridge that brings them back into connection with themselves, with others, and with the world around them.

> *"Did you ever notice that the family dog is the only animal that doesn't have to work for a living? A hen has to lay eggs, a cow has to give milk, and a canary has to sing. But a dog makes its living by giving you nothing but love."*
>
> — Dale Carnegie

💜 WHAT DOGS GIVE US	🐾 WHAT THEY ASK OF US
Loyal companionship	Daily walks, feeding, vet care
A reason to connect with others	Time, patience, and structure
Emotional support and play	Travel and housing considerations
Joyful routines and outdoor movement	Financial costs and long-term commitment

Why Dogs Help Us Feel Less Alone

There's a reason why therapy dogs are brought into hospitals, college campuses, and disaster zones: dogs regulate our nervous systems. Just petting a dog can lower cortisol levels and boost feel-good hormones like oxytocin and dopamine.

But the magic of dogs goes beyond biology. They create rhythm, routine, and opportunities for connection that many people might not otherwise have.

Daily walks become casual hellos. Dog parks become unexpected conversation starters. Even sitting on a bench with your dog invites people to stop, smile, and ask your dog's name.

It's not just the leash that brings you out of the house. It's the permission to be seen, approached, and welcomed.

Dogs and Interpersonal Synchrony

As you explored earlier in the book, connection is a rhythm. It's the invisible alignment of energy, presence, and emotional resonance.

Dogs tap into that rhythm effortlessly. They mirror your emotions. Sense your mood. Sit beside you when you're falling apart and nudge you playfully when you've forgotten how to smile.

In some ways, they're the original practitioners of empathic presence. No judgment. No words. Just warmth.

Dogs often become the bridge to human connection, gently guiding us back to social spaces we might otherwise avoid.

How Dogs Open Doors to Connection

Social Icebreakers: Taking your dog for a walk often sparks casual conversations with neighbors or fellow dog owners. People naturally feel more approachable when a wagging tail is involved.

Example: Maya, a young professional, adopted her golden retriever, Luna, to combat the isolation of working from home. Within weeks, her regular visits to the dog park led to a friendship with another dog owner. They began meeting for walks, and what started as small talk grew into a meaningful connection.

Building Community: Dogs can connect you to broader communities, from local dog parks to training classes or online groups. These spaces offer opportunities to meet like-minded people who share your love for animals.

Example: Eduardo, a recent retiree, joined a dog obedience class after adopting his German Shepherd, Max. He found not only a well-trained companion but also a group of friends who shared his interest in canine care.

Samantha's Story: The Reluctant Dog Mom

Samantha didn't plan on getting a dog. But after her daughter left for college, the house was too quiet. She missed the daily chaos, the built-in conversations, the sense of being needed.

Her friend gently suggested, "Why not foster a dog, just temporarily?"

Enter Louie. A graying rescue mutt with more anxiety than charm at first. But Louie needed her. He needed walks, meals, and medicine.

And before she knew it, Samantha had a reason to get out of the house. A reason to explore the neighborhood. A reason to linger in the park where other dog owners chatted like old friends, even though they'd only just met.

Now, Louie's was hers for good. And Samantha has more than a dog; she has a community of humans too.

She found renewed purpose in caring for Louie. The daily walks and knowing he relied on her gave Samantha the strength to rebuild her life with fresh meaning.

Caring for a dog creates a sense of responsibility that can be deeply fulfilling.

Feeling Needed: Dogs depend on you for everything: food, exercise, affection, and medical care. This reliance fosters a sense of purpose and reminds you that you're valuable in someone's life.

The Joy of Nurturing: Providing love and care to a dog creates a reciprocal bond. The joy of seeing a wagging tail when you walk through the door is a powerful antidote to loneliness.

Studies show that people who played with their pet dogs felt happier and less anxious than people who did other relaxing activities like coloring or simply sitting quietly. In fact, hanging out with your pet dog for a few minutes can make you feel better, especially after something stressful. No fancy tools or therapies needed!

What is it about dogs that makes them such incredible companions?

1. Emotional Connection

Interacting with a dog releases **oxytocin**, often referred to as the "love hormone," which promotes feelings of trust, bonding, and happiness. At the same time, **cortisol levels**, associated with stress, are significantly reduced. Just spending a few minutes petting a dog can create a calming, grounding effect that helps ease anxiety and tension.

2. Boosting Routine and Activity

Dogs thrive on structure, and caring for one naturally creates routines for feeding, walking, and playtime. This consistency doesn't just keep your dog happy; it anchors your day. Regular walks, even when you don't feel like it, encourage physical activity and fresh air, both of which are proven to improve mood and mental clarity.

3. Encouraging Mindfulness

Dogs live fully in the present moment. They're not worried about tomorrow's to-do list or yesterday's regrets. When you spend time with a dog, you're pulled into their world: watching them chase a ball, feel the wind in their fur, or nap contentedly by your side. It's a simple, powerful lesson in mindfulness. They remind you to focus on **what's happening right now**. Whether it's a walk in the park or the sound of their tail thumping happily against the floor. This ability to be present reduces stress, quiets overthinking, and helps you appreciate life's small, beautiful moments.

4. Unconditional Love

Unlike human relationships, where misunderstandings or judgments can create tension, dogs offer unwavering affection. They don't care how you look, what you've achieved, or whether you've had a bad day. They love you exactly as you are, creating a profound sense of emotional safety and connection.

Balanced Energy: A Lesson from Our Dogs

Dogs have an incredible ability to sense and respond to the energy we project. When we are balanced, calm, present, and grounded, dogs naturally mirror that energy. They trust us, relax, and become the steady companions we need.

This is one of the quiet but profound ways dogs help us heal loneliness. They don't just love us unconditionally, they teach us to become more aware of ourselves and our energy. When we're stressed, anxious, or distracted, dogs pick up on that. But the moment we shift—when we take a deep breath, focus on them, and let go of our worries—something changes. They settle, and so do we.

This dynamic is a powerful lesson in achieving balance. It starts with small moments: the mindfulness of walking a dog, the simplicity of tossing a ball, or the comfort of sitting quietly with a loyal friend curled up beside you. In those moments, our emotional energy becomes more centered, and we project calm, open vibes that not only help us connect with our dogs but also teach us how to connect with other people.

But here's the thing: **the calm, positive energy dogs bring into our lives isn't just for them. It's something we can share with others too.** How we carry ourselves, the energy we project, and how we show up in the world can transform how we connect with the people around us.

The research on the "Pet Effect" isn't totally clear yet, but a lot of people believe that having pets can really boost our well-being and health. It makes sense to think that getting a dog can help many folks by easing the loneliness.

Dogs aren't just pets; they're companions, teachers, and bridges to the world. They remind us to slow down, embrace the present moment, and find joy in the little things. Whether it's the wag of a tail, a playful bark, or the quiet comfort of their presence, dogs have a way of filling the empty spaces in our lives with love and purpose.

As much as dogs give us emotionally, they also ask something in return. If you're considering bringing a dog into your life, it's important to pause, breathe, and make sure the timing and circumstances are right for both of you.

Practical Considerations
Could a Dog Be Right for You?

Getting a dog can be life-changing, but it's not the right step for everyone. Dogs are loving companions, but they're also a daily responsibility that lasts for years. Before you fall for a pair of soulful eyes at the shelter or dive into breed research online, take a thoughtful look at your lifestyle, resources, and long-term plans.

Financial Commitment

Dogs aren't just emotionally expensive; they come with real costs. Food, grooming, vet visits, vaccinations, flea/tick prevention, toys, and bedding add up fast. Emergencies, such as a surprise surgery or a chronic illness, can strain a budget.

Tip: Ask yourself, "Can I set aside $100–$200 per month, consistently, for dog-related expenses?" If the answer feels shaky, it may be worth waiting or exploring pet insurance options in advance.

Time and Training

Even well-mannered dogs need daily structure, attention, and enrichment. Puppies, rescues, and energetic breeds may require more than love; they need training, patience, and consistency. Without it, behavioral challenges can develop that add stress rather than relief to your life.

A dog who knows how to greet guests politely, walk calmly on a leash, and respond to basic cues like "sit" or "stay" is a joy to have around. They can be part of your everyday routines, welcoming friends, tagging along for errands, or joining you on a hike, without chaos or frustration.

On the other hand, dogs who haven't learned these skills may jump on visitors, pull on the leash, bark excessively, or struggle around other dogs or children. These behaviors, while normal at first, can lead to tension in your home and even isolation if left unaddressed.

The good news? Most dogs want to learn. They just need the right guidance, repetition, and support from you.

Tip: Consider whether you have the time and emotional bandwidth to teach, reinforce, and occasionally clean up after a furry learner. If not, consider fostering first. It's a great way to learn your limits and gain experience without long-term pressure. You can also invest in positive-reinforcement classes or work with a certified trainer to get support early on. A little effort in the beginning can lead to years of shared joy and ease.

Walks and Exercise

Every dog, no matter the breed or size, needs regular movement. Walks aren't just bathroom breaks; they're essential for a dog's physical health, mental stimulation, and emotional balance. A stroll around the block or a nature trail lets your dog sniff, explore, and engage with the world in a way that toys and indoor play just can't match.

Even if you have a backyard, it's not a substitute for walks. Dogs may run a few laps outside, but they tend to wait for human engagement to feel fulfilled. A backyard provides space, but it doesn't offer the novelty, socialization, or sensory enrichment that a walk does. Without this stimulation, even dogs with access to yards can become bored or frustrated.

A well-exercised dog is often a well-behaved dog. Movement helps release pent-up energy that might otherwise show up as chewing, digging, barking, or zooming through the house. It also supports better sleep, improved focus during training, and a more relaxed temperament.

Walks also reinforce your bond. They provide predictable rhythm and structure, two things dogs love. On a walk, you're not just exercising your dog's body; you're strengthening your connection as their trusted guide.

Tip: Ask yourself honestly: can you commit to at least two walks a day, even on busy or bad-weather days? If that feels hard, consider hiring a dog walker, enrolling in a doggy daycare, or choosing a breed with lower exercise needs. Regular walks aren't a luxury. They're a daily requirement for your dog's well-being and your shared peace of mind.

Travel and Flexibility

Spontaneous weekend trips? Late nights out? Dogs rely on routine and require someone to feed, walk, and care for them if you're away. If you travel frequently for work or pleasure, you'll need a plan for pet care: friends, family, or reliable sitters.

Tip: Create a go-to care plan before you adopt. This reduces future stress and ensures your dog won't feel like an afterthought when life picks up speed.

Housing and Space

Your living situation plays a big role in your dog's happiness and yours. Some breeds need room to run; others thrive in apartments. Landlord rules, pet deposits, and breed restrictions can also shape your options.

Tip: Before committing, verify that your housing situation allows dogs and consider your long-term plans. Will your next move accommodate your pup?

Lifestyle Fit and Energy Matching

A mismatch between your energy and your dog's needs can strain the relationship. If you love long hikes, a mellow lapdog may frustrate you. If you prefer quiet nights in, a high-energy herding breed might overwhelm you.

Tip: Think in terms of compatibility. It's not about finding the "best" dog, but the best dog for your lifestyle, personality, and preferences.

Long-Term Vision

Dogs live 10–15 years on average. Adopting a dog isn't just about today, it's about your next decade. Careers shift. Relationships change. Life throws curveballs. Are you prepared to keep showing up for a pet who'll depend on you the whole time?

Tip: If the idea of committing for the long haul excites you more than it scares you, you might be ready.

Choose the Right Match

Finding the right dog isn't just about breed or cuteness; it's about alignment. A good match considers energy, environment, personality, and your everyday life. The more honestly you assess your needs and routines, the better your chances of building a connection that feels natural and nourishing for both of you.

Energy Levels

Do you crave outdoor adventures or quiet evenings on the couch? A high-energy dog might be perfect for someone who loves hiking, running, or frequent playtime. On the other hand, a calmer breed may be ideal for slower-paced lifestyles or smaller homes.

Tip: If you're already active, a dog can become your favorite workout partner. If not, a mellow companion may be better suited to your rhythm.

Size Matters

Larger dogs often need more space to move and stretch, while smaller breeds can feel right at home in an apartment. That said, energy, not size, is often the bigger factor. Some small dogs have huge energy; some big dogs just want to nap.

Tip: Consider your living space, access to outdoor areas, and how much daily movement your routine allows.

Personality Fit

Think about your temperament. Are you patient, affectionate, and consistent? Do you want a snuggler, a shadow, or a social butterfly? Dogs, like people, have different love languages. Matching personalities can make life together feel joyful instead of stressful.

Tip: If you're sensitive to noise or mess, avoid breeds known for barking or shedding. If you're nurturing, consider a dog that thrives on close companionship.

Lifestyle Compatibility

Night owl or early bird? Homebody or frequent traveler? Couch cuddler or weekend warrior? Every dog thrives on predictability. The best fit is a dog who can thrive within the contours of your normal days.

Tip: Imagine your typical week. Can you consistently offer walks, attention, and care? The best match doesn't change your life; it gently enhances it.

Adoption or Breeder? Start with Heart

Shelters and rescue organizations are full of dogs waiting for loving homes. Adopting a dog can be an incredibly meaningful way to welcome connection into your life, not only for you, but for them. Whether you choose a rescue or a breeder, start with heart, and choose with care. What matters most is not where your dog comes from, but the life you build together.

Can't Have a Dog? Connection Is Still Possible

Not everyone can or should adopt a pet and that's okay. But there are still ways to experience the dog effect in your life:

- Volunteer at a local animal shelter (many need walkers and cuddling companions)
- Join a dog-walking or pet-sitting app (like Rover or Wag)
- Offer to help a friend or neighbor care for their dog
- Visit dog parks as a guest. People love talking about their pets
- Attend pet-friendly community events where connection naturally unfolds

Dogs are connection magnets. Even when they're not your own, they have a way of opening hearts and starting conversations that otherwise wouldn't happen.

What This Means: Friendship doesn't always start with another person. Sometimes, it begins with a wagging tail, a walk around the block, and a moment of shared joy that reminds you you're part of something.

Why It Matters: Loneliness thrives in silence and stillness. Dogs interrupt both. They give us purpose, routine, and a reason to open our door (and our hearts) just a little more each day.

What Comes Next: If you're feeling disconnected, consider starting with a dog. Not just for the cuddles, but for the community they create.

And if a dog isn't an option?

Start where dogs tend to thrive: **in presence, playfulness, and consistency.** Those three qualities are at the heart of every great connection—furry or not.

Dogs don't care if you're a mess.
They'll sit in the mess with you
and wag their tail like you're doing just fine.

What's Your Canine Connection Style?

This playful, introspective quiz is designed to help you explore your personality and daily rhythm—and find a dog whose temperament and size align with your life.

Circle your answers, total the letters, and explore your recommended matches.

1. Your ideal Saturday afternoon:

- (a) Hiking, jogging, or exploring the outdoors
- (b) Reading, relaxing, or enjoying quiet activities
- (c) Hosting brunch or catching up with friends
- (d) Volunteering, helping family, or checking in with loved ones

2. Your home is best described as:

- (a) Buzzing with activity—lots of motion
- (b) Calm, cozy, and quiet
- (c) Social and lively
- (d) Warm, dependable, and nurturing

3. Your approach to challenges is usually:

- (a) Jump in and power through
- (b) Stay grounded and think before acting
- (c) Talk it through and process with others
- (d) Offer support before asking for any

4. What grounds and recharges you?

(a) Movement—walks, workouts, or physical tasks

(b) Stillness—meditation, journaling, or quiet moments

(c) Togetherness—connection, laughter, conversation

(d) Purpose—being needed, nurturing others

5. Your friendships are marked by:

(a) Spontaneity and shared adventures

(b) Loyalty and emotional presence

(c) Playfulness and connection

(d) Compassion and protectiveness

Results: Your Match by Energy and Size

Mostly A's – The Adventurer: You thrive on motion, nature, and staying active. Look for an athletic dog who can keep up with your pace and loves exploring.

- **Small Breeds:** Jack Russell Terrier, Miniature Pinscher
- **Medium Breeds:** Border Collie, Australian Shepherd
- **Large Breeds:** Labrador Retriever, German Shorthaired Pointer, Belgian Malinois

Mostly B's – The Soulful Companion: You value peace, reflection, and grounded presence. You'll bond best with a gentle dog who mirrors your calm and provides companionship without chaos.

- **Small Breeds:** Italian Greyhound, Cavalier King Charles Spaniel
- **Medium Breeds:** Whippet, Standard Poodle
- **Large Breeds:** Greyhound, Bernese Mountain Dog

Mostly C's – The Social Butterfly: You're expressive, friendly, and love shared joy. You'll enjoy a dog that's cheerful, sociable, and ready to greet the world with a wag.

- **Small Breeds:** Cocker Spaniel, Havanese
- **Medium Breeds:** Beagle, French Bulldog
- **Large Breeds:** Golden Retriever, Boxer

Mostly D's – The Heart Guardian: You're nurturing and protective, with a strong sense of purpose. You'll thrive with a dog who bonds deeply and may need a little extra love, patience, or purpose.

- **Small Breeds:** Shih Tzu (especially seniors or rescues), Pekingese
- **Medium Breeds:** Rescue mixes with medical/emotional needs, Basset Hound
- **Large Breeds:** Great Pyrenees, Mastiff, older shelter dogs needing second chances

IMPORTANT FOOTNOTE:

Every dog is unique.

While breed traits offer helpful generalizations, they do not define a dog's personality or needs. Temperament, energy, and behavior vary widely—even within a breed. The most reliable way to know if a dog is the right fit is to meet them in person, spend time together, and talk to rescue staff, breeders, or fosters who know them well.

For helpful tools, books, and expert guidance on choosing the right dog, see the list of recommended resources in Part 4.

Part 4

Resources and References

Recommended Resources

Bibliography

Want More?
Download your free college friendship guide

Let's Stay in Touch

About the Author

Recommended Resources

Over the years, I've come across books, podcasts, and tools that didn't just inform me—they helped shape the way I think, connect, and lead. These aren't just popular titles or trendy shows. They're resources I've personally leaned on, recommended to clients, and returned to during different seasons of growth. Whether you're navigating relationships, building confidence, or simply seeking a deeper understanding, I hope you'll find something here that sparks clarity, comfort, or curiosity. This list is not about perfection or influence—it's about real conversations and grounded wisdom that have made a difference for me, and might do the same for you.

If you've read the chapters about building connection and finding the right people for your life, you already know this book is about more than human relationships—it's about meaningful bonds in every form. For many of us, adopting a dog becomes one of the most rewarding ways to experience unconditional connection. Whether you're thinking about bringing a dog into your life or just curious about how to find the right fit, I wanted to share some tools and resources that can guide you through the process with heart, clarity, and responsibility. These aren't just how-to guides—they're about alignment, lifestyle, and love. Because choosing a dog, much like choosing the people we surround ourselves with, deserves thought and care.

Top 5 Must-Reads for Confidence, Clarity and Connection

- *Let Them Theory* – Mel Robbins (2024)
  A viral, liberating mindset shift: let people do what they do—and free yourself to be who you are.

- *Think Like a Monk* – Jay Shetty (2020)
  Modern wisdom for creating inner peace, purpose, and connection.

- *Chatter* – Ethan Kross (2021)
  How to stop your inner critic from hijacking your mood, decisions, and confidence.

- *Captivate* – Vanessa Van Edwards (2017)
  Science-backed strategies to make meaningful first impressions and social connections.

- *Gifts of Imperfection* – Brené Brown (2010)
  A foundational guide for letting go of expectations and embracing authentic living.

Expanded Recommended Reading

Mindset, Motivation and Personal Growth

- *Atomic Habits* – James Clear (2018)
  The ripple effect of small changes that lead to transformative results.

- *Authenticity Principle* – Ritu Bhasin (2017)
  A call to live and lead more freely, breaking free from external expectations.

- *High 5 Habit* – Mel Robbins (2021)
  A daily self-affirmation ritual that boosts confidence and self-connection.

Connection, Communication and Confidence

- *Cues* – Vanessa Van Edwards (2022)
  Learn 96 nonverbal signals to build trust, connection, and influence.

- *How to Win Friends and Influence People* – Dale Carnegie (1936)
  Still relevant, still powerful: the original guide to building rapport.

- *Likeability Trap* – Alicia Menendez (2019)
  Explores how women can escape the double bind between being liked and being respected.

Inner Dialogue, Psychology and the Brain

- *Self-Compassion* – Kristin Neff (2011)
  Science-backed tools for replacing self-criticism with kindness and motivation.

- *Useful Delusions* – Shankar Vedantam and Bill Mesler (2021)
  Why some forms of self-deception help us live more connected, meaningful lives.

Recommended Podcasts

These podcasts go deeper into the themes explored throughout the book—connection, communication, inner dialogue, and belonging. Here are some standout episodes to start with:

The Happiness Lab with Dr. Laurie Santos
www.happinesslab.fm

- *Stepping Off the Path of Anxiety* – Andrea Wachter
- *Feel Like You're Enough* – Dr. Ellen Hendriksen
- *Friendship Roundtable* – Gretchen Rubin & Reshma Saujani
- *The Secret to Making Friends as an Adult* – Dr. Marisa Franco

Hidden Brain with Shankar Vedantam
www.hiddenbrain.org

- *How Others See You* – Dr. Erica Boothby
- *The Gift of Other People* – Dr. Nicholas Epley
- *How to Win People Over* – Dr. Alison Fragale
- *You 2.0: Befriending Your Inner Voice* – Dr. Ethan Kross
- *Relationships 2.0: An Antidote to Loneliness* – Dr. Vivek Murthy

Huberman Lab

www.hubermanlab.com

- *How Smartphones & Social Media Impact Mental Health* – Dr. Jonathan Haidt
- *Science of Social Bonding in Family, Friendship & Romantic Love*
- *Science-Based Tools for Increasing Happiness*

Mel Robbins Podcast

www.melrobbins.com/podcast

- *Let Them Theory: The Life Advice That's Gone Viral for a Reason*
- *It's Not You: The Real Reason Adult Friendship Is So Hard* – Danielle Bayard Jackson
- *5 Things Only Fake Friends Do & How to Let Go of What No Longer Serves You* – Trent Shelton

On Purpose with Jay Shetty

www.jayshetty.me/podcast

- *Stop Overthinking Every Social Interaction!* – Vanessa Van Edwards
- *8 Ways to Decide Which Friendships to Invest In & Which to Let Go*
- *7+ Powerful Habits to Avoid Loneliness & Build Authentic Community*

Choosing the Right Dog

Websites and Tools

- **Petfinder.com** – Search adoptable dogs by breed, size, age, and temperament near you.
- **AKC dog breed selector tool** – A lifestyle-based quiz to match you with suitable breeds.
  https://www.akc.org/breed-selector-tool/
- **Rescue organizations and local shelters** – Many offer "foster-to-adopt" options so you can trial the fit.
- **Certified professional dog trainers** – Useful for behavioral evaluations and pre-adoption consultations.

Books on Choosing the Right Dog

By Cesar Millan

- *Cesar's Way* – Cesar Millan
- *A Member of the Family* – Cesar Millan
- *How to Raise the Perfect Dog* – Cesar Millan
- *The Dog Selector* – David Alderton
- *Decoding Your Dog* – American College of Veterinary Behaviorists

Reminder:

Breed characteristics can offer helpful guidelines, but every dog is a unique individual. The best way to ensure a good match is to meet the dog, ask lots of questions, observe behavior, and spend time together before committing.

Bibliography

Here are some books, studies, and sources that have really influenced the ideas in this book. Some helped me lay the groundwork for my research, while others provided the perfect words for experiences I've noticed but couldn't quite name. I'm so thankful for the incredible people behind this work—their insights have helped me connect the dots and share something meaningful with you.

Albano, A. M., & DiBartolo, P. M. (2007). *Cognitive-behavioral therapy for social phobia in adolescents: Stand up, speak out*. Oxford University Press.

American Psychiatric Association. (2022). *Diagnostic and statistical manual of mental disorders* (5th ed., text rev.; DSM-5-TR). American Psychiatric Publishing.

American Psychological Association. (2023, May). The science of why friendships keep us healthy. *Monitor on Psychology*. https://www.apa.org/monitor/2023/05/friendships-health

Antony, M. M., & Swinson, R. P. (2008). *The shyness and social anxiety workbook: Proven, step-by-step techniques for overcoming your fear* (2nd ed.). New Harbinger Publications.

Aron, A., Melinat, E., Aron, E. N., Vallone, R. D., & Bator, R. J. (1997). The experimental generation of interpersonal closeness. *Personality and Social Psychology Bulletin*, 23(4), 363–377.

Asher, M., Barthel, A. L., Hofmann, S. G., Okon-Singer, H., & Aderka, I. M. (2021). When two hearts beat as one: Heart-rate synchrony in social anxiety disorder. *Behaviour Research and Therapy*, 141, 103859. https://doi.org/10.1016/j.brat.2021.103859

Beck, A. T. (1976). *Cognitive therapy and the emotional disorders*. International Universities Press.

Bernieri, F. J., & Rosenthal, R. (1991). Interpersonal coordination: Behavior matching and interactional synchrony. In R. S. Feldman & B. Rime (Eds.), *Fundamentals of nonverbal behavior* (pp. 401–432). Cambridge University Press.

Bhasin, R. (2023). *We've got this: Unlocking the beauty of belonging*. Amplify Publishing.

Bhaskhar, N. (2020). *Understanding your cognitive distortions*. Stanford University. https://web.stanford.edu/~nanbhas/blog/understanding-cognitive-distortions/

Boothby, E. J., Cooney, G., Sandstrom, G. M., & Clark, M. S. (2018). The liking gap in conversations: Do people like us more than we think? *Psychological Science*, 29(11), 1742–1756. https://doi.org/10.1177/0956797618783714

Branden, N. (1994). *The six pillars of self-esteem*. Bantam.

Breines, J. G., & Chen, S. (2012). Self-compassion increases self-improvement motivation. *Personality and Social Psychology Bulletin, 38*(9), 1133–1143. https://doi.org/10.1177/0146167212445599

Brown, B. (2012). *Daring greatly: How the courage to be vulnerable transforms the way we live, love, parent, and lead*. Gotham Books.

Burns, D. D. (1980). *Feeling good: The new mood therapy*. William Morrow and Company.

Burns, D. D. (1999). *The feeling good handbook*. Plume.

Cacioppo, J. T., & Cacioppo, S. (2018). Loneliness in the modern age: An evolutionary theory of loneliness (ETL). *Advances in experimental social psychology* (Vol. 58, pp. 127–197). Academic Press. https://doi.org/10.1016/bs.aesp.2018.03.003

Cacioppo, J. T., & Patrick, W. (2008). *Loneliness: Human nature and the need for social connection*. W. W. Norton & Company.

Campo, R. A., & Uchino, B. N. (2013). Humans' bonding with their companion dogs: Cardiovascular benefits during and after stress. *Journal of Sociology and Social Welfare, 40*(4), 237–259. https://doi.org/10.15453/0191-5096.3769

Carnegie, D. (2022). *How to win friends and influence people* (Reissue ed.). Simon & Schuster.

Centers for Disease Control and Prevention. (2023, May 8). *Loneliness and social isolation linked to serious health conditions*. U.S. Department of Health and Human Services. https://www.cdc.gov/aging/publications/features/lonely-older-adults.html

Christian, H., Bauman, A., Epping, J. N., Levine, G. N., McCormack, G., Rhodes, R. E., ... & Westgarth, C. (2018). Encouraging dog walking for health promotion and disease prevention. *American Journal of Lifestyle Medicine, 12*(3), 233–243. https://doi.org/10.1177/1559827616643686

Clark, D. M., & Wells, A. (1995). Recent advances in the understanding and psychological treatment of social anxiety disorder. *Behaviour Research and Therapy, 37*(4), 319–345. https://doi.org/10.1016/S0005-7967(98)00060-7

Cooney, G., Boothby, E. J., & Lee, M. (2022). The thought gap after conversation: Underestimating the frequency of others' thoughts about us. *Journal of Experimental Psychology: General, 151*(5), 1069–1088. https://doi.org/10.1037/xge0001134

Cozolino, L. (2014). *The neuroscience of human relationships: Attachment and the developing social brain* (2nd ed.). W. W. Norton & Company.

Crossman, M. K., Kazdin, A. E., Matijczak, A., Kitt, R. E., & Santos, L. R. (2018). The influence of interactions with dogs on affect, anxiety, and arousal in children. *Journal of Clinical Child & Adolescent Psychology, 47*(5), 754–764. https://doi.org/10.1080/15374416.2018.1520119

Cuddy, A. (2015). *Presence: Bringing your boldest self to your biggest challenges.* Little, Brown and Company.

Dijk, C., Fischer, A. H., Morina, N., van Eeuwijk, C., & van Kleef, G. A. (2018). Effects of social anxiety on emotional mimicry and contagion: Feeling negative, but smiling politely. *Journal of Nonverbal Behavior, 42*(1), 81–99. https://doi.org/10.1007/s10919-017-0266-z

Dikker, S., Wan, L., Davidesco, I., Kaggen, L., Oostrik, M., McClintock, J., Rowland, J., Michalareas, G., Van Bavel, J. J., Ding, M., & Poeppel, D. (2017). Brain-to-brain synchrony tracks real-world dynamic group interactions in the classroom. *Current Biology, 27*(9), 1375–1380. https://doi.org/10.1016/j.cub.2017.04.002

Dunbar, R. I. M. (2018). The anatomy of friendship. *Trends in Cognitive Sciences, 22*(1), 32–51. https://doi.org/10.1016/j.tics.2017.10.004

Ekman, P. (2003). *Emotions revealed: Recognizing faces and feelings to improve communication and emotional life.* Times Books.

Epley, N. (2014). *Mindwise: Why we misunderstand what others think, believe, feel, and want.* Knopf.

Epley, N., & Schroeder, J. (2014). Mistakenly seeking solitude. *Journal of Experimental Psychology: General, 143*(5), 1980–1999. https://doi.org/10.1037/a0037323

Feldman, R. (2007). Parent-infant synchrony: Biological foundations and developmental outcomes. *Current Directions in Psychological Science, 16*(6), 340–345. https://doi.org/10.1111/j.1467-8721.2007.00532.x

Feldman, R. (2012). Parent–infant synchrony: A biopsychosocial model of mutual influences in the formation of affiliative bonds. *Monographs of the Society for Research in Child Development, 77*(2), 42–51. https://doi.org/10.1111/j.1540-5834.2011.00660.x

Fredrickson, B. L. (2001). The role of positive emotions in positive psychology: The broaden-and-build theory of positive emotions. *American Psychologist, 56*(3), 218–226. https://doi.org/10.1037/0003-066X.56.3.218

Frontiers in Psychology. (2022). The components of interpersonal synchrony in the typical population. *Frontiers in Psychology.* https://www.frontiersin.org/articles/10.3389/fpsyg.2022.850765/full

Fugazza, C., Pogány, Á., & Miklósi, Á. (2016). Social learning in dog training: The effectiveness of the Do as I Do method compared to shaping/clicker training. *Applied Animal Behaviour Science, 171,* 146–151. https://doi.org/10.1016/j.applanim.2015.08.033

Gabor, D. (2011). *How to start a conversation and make friends* (Rev. and updated ed.). Fireside.

Gazipura, A. (2013). *The solution to social anxiety: Break free from the shyness that holds you back.* Center for Social Confidence.

Gilovich, T., Medvec, V. H., & Savitsky, K. (2000). The spotlight effect in social judgment: An egocentric bias in estimates of the salience of one's own actions and appearance. *Journal of Personality and Social Psychology, 78*(2), 211–222. https://doi.org/10.1037/0022-3514.78.2.211

Goleman, D. (1995). *Emotional intelligence: Why it can matter more than IQ.* Bantam Books.

Goleman, D. (2006). *Social intelligence: The revolutionary new science of human relationships*. Bantam Books.

Goman, C. K. (2008). *The nonverbal advantage: Secrets and science of body language at work*. Berrett-Koehler.

Greater Good Science Center. (2014). Social connection in *"The Science of Happiness"*. University of California, Berkeley. https://greatergood.berkeley.edu/article/item/the_science_of_happiness

Haferkamp, N., & Krämer, N. C. (2011). Social comparison 2.0: Examining the effects of online profiles on social-networking sites. *Cyberpsychology, Behavior, and Social Networking, 14*(5), 309–314. https://doi.org/10.1089/cyber.2010.0120

Haidt, J. (2006). *The happiness hypothesis: Finding modern truth in ancient wisdom*. Basic Books.

Haidt, J. (2024). *The anxious generation: How the great rewiring of childhood is causing an epidemic of mental illness*. Penguin Press.

Hall, J. A. (2019). How many hours does it take to make a friend? *Journal of Social and Personal Relationships, 36*(4), 1278–1296.

Handlin, L., Hydbring-Sandberg, E., Nilsson, A., Ejdebäck, M., Jansson, A., & Uvnäs-Moberg, K. (2011). Short-term interaction between dogs and their owners: Effects on oxytocin, cortisol, insulin and heart rate—An exploratory study. *Anthrozoös, 24*(3), 301–315. https://doi.org/10.2752/175303711X13045914865385

Hare, B., & Woods, V. (2013). *The genius of dogs: How dogs are smarter than you think*. Dutton.

Hatfield, E., Cacioppo, J. T., & Rapson, R. L. (1994). *Emotional contagion*. Cambridge University Press.

Hendrikse, S. C. F., Treur, J., Wilderjans, T. F., Dikker, S., & Koole, S. L. (2023). On becoming in sync with yourself and others: An adaptive agent model for how persons connect by detecting intrapersonal and interpersonal synchrony. *Human-Centric Intelligent Systems, 3*(1), 123–146. https://doi.org/10.1007/s44230-023-00019-1

Hope, N., Koestner, R., & Milyavskaya, M. (2014). The role of self-compassion in goal pursuit and well-being among university freshmen. *Self and Identity, 13*(5), 579–593. https://doi.org/10.1080/15298868.2014.889032

Huberman, A. (Host). (2021, December 20). *Science of social bonding in family, friendship & romantic love* [Audio podcast episode]. In *Huberman Lab Podcast*. Scicomm Media. https://www.hubermanlab.com/episode/science-of-social-bonding-in-family-friendship-and-romantic-love

Huberman, A. (Host). (2022, November 14). *Science-based tools for increasing happiness* [Audio podcast episode]. In *Huberman Lab Podcast*. https://hubermanlab.com/episode/science-based-tools-for-increasing-happiness

Huberman, A. (Host). (2024, February 5). *Dr. Kay Tye: The Biology of Social Interactions and Emotions* [Audio podcast episode]. In *Huberman Lab Podcast*. https://www.hubermanlab.com/episode/dr-kay-tye-the-biology-of-social-interactions-and-emotions

Huberman, A. (Host). (2024, June 10). *Dr. Jonathan Haidt: How Smartphones & Social Media Impact Mental Health & the Realistic Solutions* [Audio podcast episode]. In *Huberman Lab Podcast*. https://www.hubermanlab.com/episode/dr-jonathan-haidt-how-smartphones-social-media-impact-mental-health-the-realistic-solutions

Huberman, A. (Host). (2024, October 15). *What's going on with your social anxiety?* [Audio podcast episode]. In *Huberman Lab Podcast*. https://ai.hubermanlab.com/d/f35f10a2-7b29-11ef-9724-97d30ba87089

Huberman, A. (Host). (2024, December 23). *Dr. Laurie Santos: How to achieve true happiness using science-based protocols* [Audio podcast episode]. In *Huberman Lab Podcast*. Scicomm Media. https://www.hubermanlab.com/episode/dr-laurie-santos-how-to-achieve-true-happiness-using-science-based-protocols

Huberman, A. (Host). (2025, April 28). *What Pets Actually Want & Need (guest Dr. Karolina Westlund)* [Audio podcast episode]. In *Huberman Lab Podcast*. Scicomm Media. https://www.hubermanlab.com/episode/understand-what-pets-actually-want-need-dr-karolina-westlund

Jiang, J. (2012, November 15). Day 1: Asking to borrow $100 from a stranger. *Rejection Therapy*. https://www.rejectiontherapy.com/blog/2012/11/15/the-100-days-rejection-therapy

Iacoboni, M. (2009). *Mirroring people: The new science of how we connect with others*. Picador.

Insel, T. R. (2010). The challenge of translation in social neuroscience: A review of oxytocin, vasopressin, and affiliative behavior. *Neuron, 65*(6), 768–779. https://doi.org/10.1016/j.neuron.2010.03.005

Killam, K. (2024). *The art and science of connection*. HarperCollins.

Kocovski, N. L., Fleming, J. E., & Rector, N. A. (2009). The impact of cognitive restructuring and mindfulness strategies on post-event processing and affect in social anxiety. *Journal of Anxiety Disorders, 23*(3), 371–376. https://doi.org/10.1016/j.janxdis.2008.12.006

Kramer, J., Conner, B. T., & Barrett, M. S. (2016). What works in preventing emerging social anxiety: Exposure and cognitive restructuring. *Journal of Anxiety Disorders, 40*, 41–47. https://doi.org/10.1016/j.janxdis.2016.04.001

Kross, E. (2021). *Chatter: The voice in our head, why it matters, and how to harness it*. Crown Publishing Group.

Kumar, A., & Epley, N. (2021). A little good goes an unexpectedly long way: Underestimating the positive impact of kindness on recipients. *Journal of Experimental Psychology: General, 150*(8), 1645–1660. https://doi.org/10.1037/xge0001041

Lieberman, M. D. (2013). *Social: Why our brains are wired to connect*. Crown Publishing Group.

Lumsden, J., Miles, L. K., & Macrae, C. N. (2014). Sync or sink? Interpersonal synchrony impacts self-esteem. *Frontiers in Psychology, 5*, 1064. https://doi.org/10.3389/fpsyg.2014.01064

MacLean, E. L., & Hare, B. (2015). Dogs hijack the human bonding pathway. *Science, 348*(6232), 280–281. https://doi.org/10.1126/science.aaa6400

Matijczak, A., Yates, M. S., Ruiz, M. C., Santos, L. R., Kazdin, A. E., & Raila, H. (2023). The influence of interactions with pet dogs on psychological distress. *Emotion, 24*(2), 384–396. https://doi.org/10.1037/emo0001256

Mayo, O., & Gordon, I. (2020). In and out of synchrony—Behavioral and physiological dynamics of dyadic interpersonal coordination. *Psychophysiology, 57*(6), e13574. https://doi.org/10.1111/psyp.13574

McNicholas, J., Gilbey, A., Rennie, A., Ahmedzai, S., Dono, J. A., & Ormerod, E. (2005). Pet ownership and human health: A brief review of evidence and issues. *BMJ, 331*(7527), 1252–1254. https://doi.org/10.1136/bmj.331.7527.1252

Murthy, V. H. (2020). *Together: The healing power of human connection in a sometimes lonely world.* Harper Wave.

Murthy, V. H. (2023). *Our epidemic of loneliness and isolation: The U.S. Surgeon General's advisory on the healing effects of social connection and community.* U.S. Department of Health and Human Services. https://www.hhs.gov/sites/default/files/surgeon-general-social-connection-advisory.pdf

Navarro, J., & Karlins, M. (2008). *What every BODY is saying: An ex-FBI agent's guide to speed-reading people.* HarperCollins.

National Institute of Mental Health. (2023). *Social anxiety disorder: Statistics and facts.* U.S. Department of Health and Human Services. https://www.nimh.nih.gov/health/statistics/social-anxiety-disorder

Neff, K. D. (2011). *Self-compassion: The proven power of being kind to yourself.* William Morrow.

Neff, K. D., & Germer, C. K. (2013). A pilot study and randomized controlled trial of the mindful self-compassion program. *Journal of Clinical Psychology, 69*(1), 28–44. https://doi.org/10.1002/jclp.21923

Pease, A., & Pease, B. (2004). *The definitive book of body language.* Bantam.

Petersson, M., Uvnäs-Moberg, K., Nilsson, A., Gustafson, L. L., Hydbring-Sandberg, E., & Handlin, L. (2017). Oxytocin and cortisol levels in dog owners and their dogs are associated with behavioral patterns: An exploratory study. *Frontiers in Psychology, 8*, 1796. https://doi.org/10.3389/fpsyg.2017.01796

Porges, S. W. (2011). *The polyvagal theory: Neurophysiological foundations of emotions, attachment, communication, and self-regulation.* W. W. Norton & Company.

Powers, T. A., Koestner, R., & Zuroff, D. C. (2007). Self-criticism, goal motivation, and goal progress. *Journal of Social and Clinical Psychology, 26*(7), 826–840. https://doi.org/10.1521/jscp.2007.26.7.826

Ramseyer, F., & Tschacher, W. (2011). Nonverbal synchrony in psychotherapy: Coordinated body movement reflects relationship quality and outcome. *Journal of Consulting and Clinical Psychology, 79*(3), 284–295. https://doi.org/10.1037/a0023419

Ramseyer, F., & Tschacher, W. (2014). Nonverbal synchrony of head- and body-movement in psychotherapy: Different signals have different associations with outcome. *Frontiers in Psychology, 5*, Article 979. https://doi.org/10.3389/fpsyg.2014.00979

Rizzolatti, G., & Craighero, L. (2004). The mirror-neuron system. *Annual Review of Neuroscience, 27*, 169–192. https://doi.org/10.1146/annurev.neuro.27.070203.144230

Robbins, M. (2017). *The 5 second rule: Transform your life, work, and confidence with everyday courage.* Savio Republic.

Robbins, M. (2024). *The let them theory.* Hay House LLC.

Robbins, M. (Host). (2023, April 10). *The Let Them Theory: The life advice that's gone viral for a reason* [Audio podcast episode]. In *The Mel Robbins Podcast.* https://www.melrobbins.com/episode/episode-93/

Robbins, M. (Host). (2023, June 15). *The secret to a happy life: What the longest study on happiness reveals* [Audio podcast episode]. In *The Mel Robbins Podcast.* https://www.melrobbins.com/podcast/

Robbins, M. (Host). (2023, July 10). *Where did all my friends go? A simple guide to finding your people (steal this!)* [Audio podcast episode]. In *The Mel Robbins Podcast.* https://www.melrobbins.com/episode/episode-82/

Robbins, M. (Host). (2023, July 24). *You are a badass: Unlock your most authentic self in 4 proven steps (with Ritu Bhasin)* [Audio podcast episode]. In *The Mel Robbins Podcast.* Mel Robbins. https://www.melrobbins.com/episode/episode-86/

Robbins, M. (Host). (2024, February 29). *5 things only fake friends do & how to let go of what no longer serves you (with Trent Shelton)* [Audio podcast episode]. In *The Mel Robbins Podcast.* Mel Robbins. https://www.melrobbins.com/episode/episode-151/

Robbins, M. (Host). (2024, April 15). *If you struggle with anxiety, this episode will change your life* [Audio podcast episode]. In *The Mel Robbins Podcast.* https://www.melrobbins.com/episode/episode-41/

Robbins, M. (Host). (2024, August 24). *8 things I wish I knew in college* [Audio podcast episode]. In *The Mel Robbins Podcast.* https://www.melrobbins.com/episode/episode-207/

Robbins, M. (Host). (2025, February 10). *Why making friends as an adult feels impossible & what to do about it* [Audio podcast episode]. In The Mel Robbins Podcast. https://www.melrobbins.com/episode/episode-262/

Robbins, M. (Host). (2025, February 27). *How to Handle Difficult People & Take Back Your Peace and Power (with Jefferson Fisher)* [Audio podcast episode]. In The Mel Robbins Podcast. https://www.melrobbins.com/episode/episode-267/

Robbins, M. (Host). (2025, April 24). *It's not you: The real reason adult friendship is so hard & 3 ways to make it easier (with Danielle Bayard Jackson)* [Audio podcast episode]. In The Mel Robbins Podcast. https://www.melrobbins.com/episode/episode-283/

Romero, T., Hernández-Lallement, J., Lahoz, E., Gallardo, D., & Palagi, E. (2013). Familiarity bias and physiological responses in contagious yawning by dogs support link to empathy. *PLOS ONE, 8*(8), e71365. https://doi.org/10.1371/journal.pone.0071365

Santos, L. (Host). (2024, September 20). *Stepping off the path of anxiety* [Audio podcast episode]. In *The Happiness Lab*. Pushkin Industries. https://www.happinesslab.fm

Santos, L. (Host). (2024, February 19). *Feel like you're enough (with Dr. Ellen Hendriksen)* [Audio podcast episode]. In *The Happiness Lab*. Pushkin Industries. https://www.happinesslab.fm

Santos, L. (Host). (2024, March 25). *Friendship roundtable: How to make, keep & deepen friendships (with Gretchen Rubin & Reshma Saujani)* [Audio podcast episode]. In *The Happiness Lab*. Pushkin Industries. https://www.happinesslab.fm

Santos, L. (Host). (2023, October 30). *Mistakenly seeking solitude* [Audio podcast episode]. In *The Happiness Lab*. Pushkin Industries. https://www.happinesslab.fm

Santos, L. (Host). (2023, November 6). *The introvert's guide to extroversion* [Audio podcast episode]. In *The Happiness Lab*. Pushkin Industries. https://www.happinesslab.fm

Santos, L. (Host). (2023, October 16). *Text a friend... right now!* [Audio podcast episode]. In *The Happiness Lab*. Pushkin Industries. https://www.happinesslab.fm

Santos, L. (Host). (2023, June 20). *How talking to a friend helps (Live at The International Festival of Arts and Ideas) (with Dr. Tamar Gendler)* [Audio podcast episode]. In *The Happiness Lab*. Pushkin Industries. https://www.happinesslab.fm

Santos, L. (Host). (2023, May 22). *How to make friends and compliment people* [Audio podcast episode]. In *The Happiness Lab*. Pushkin Industries. https://www.happinesslab.fm

Santos, L. (Host). (2023, May 1). *The secret to making friends as an adult (with Dr. Marisa Franco)* [Audio podcast episode]. In *The Happiness Lab*. Pushkin Industries. https://www.happinesslab.fm

Santos, L. (Host). (2023, June 5). *Friendships: Handling change, conflict and finding new friends (with Gretchen Rubin & Reshma Saujani)* [Audio podcast episode]. In *The Happiness Lab*. Pushkin Industries. https://www.happinesslab.fm

Satyan, V. S. (2023). *Thoughts are not facts: A guide to mastering cognitive distortions.* Barnes & Noble Press.

Schroeder, J., Lyons, D., & Epley, N. (2023). Hello, stranger?: Pleasant conversations are preceded by concerns about starting one. *Journal of Experimental Psychology: General, 152*(2), 374–389. https://doi.org/10.1037/xge0001226

Shetty, J. (2020). *Think like a monk: Train your mind for peace and purpose every day.* Simon & Schuster.

Shetty, J. (2023). *8 rules of love: How to find it, keep it, and let it go.* Simon & Schuster.

Shetty, J. (Host). (2023, July 17). *Nessa Barrett ON: How to Overcome Loneliness & 8 Ways to Heal From a Breakup* [Audio podcast episode]. In *On Purpose.* https://www.jayshetty.me/podcast/nessa-barrett-on-how-to-overcome-loneliness-and-8-ways-to-heal-from-a-breakup

Shetty, J. (Host). (2023, September 1). *7+ Powerful Habits To Avoid Loneliness, Feel Connected And Build Authentic Community* [Audio podcast episode]. In *On Purpose.* https://www.jayshetty.me/podcast/7-powerful-habits-to-avoid-loneliness-feel-connected-and-build-authentic-community

Shetty, J. (Host). (2024, April 22). *8 Ways to Decide Which Friendships to Invest In & Which Friendships to Let Go Of* [Audio podcast episode]. In *On Purpose.* https://www.jayshetty.me/podcast/8-ways-to-decide-which-friendships-to-invest-in-which-friendships-to-let-go-of

Shetty, J. (Host). (2025, April 11). *Why Making New Friends Feels Exhausting As An Adult (And How to Make It Easier)* [Audio podcast episode]. In *On Purpose.* https://www.jayshetty.me/podcast/why-making-new-friends-feels-exhausting-as-an-adult-and-how-to-make-it-easier

Shetty, J. (Host). (2025, May 12). *Vanessa Van Edwards: Stop Overthinking Every Social Interaction! (Use these cues to be liked, respected, and build confidence in every conversation)* [Audio podcast episode]. In *On Purpose.* https://www.jayshetty.me/podcast/vanessa-van-edwards-stop-overthinking-every-social-interaction-use-these-cues-to-be-liked-respected-and-build-confidence

Shahin, A. J., Hu, X., Liu, Y., & Rapp, B. (2021). Behavioral synchrony and trust: An interpersonal EEG study. *Social Cognitive and Affective Neuroscience, 16*(1–2), 141–151. https://doi.org/10.1093/scan/nsaa146

Siegel, D. J. (2010). *The mindful therapist: A clinician's guide to mindsight and neural integration.* W. W. Norton & Company.

Siegel, D. J. (2012). *The developing mind: How relationships and the brain interact to shape who we are* (2nd ed.). Guilford Press.

Smeets, E., Neff, K. D., Alberts, H., & Peters, M. L. (2014). Meeting suffering with kindness: Effects of a brief self-compassion intervention for female college students. *Journal of Clinical Psychology, 70*(9), 794–807. https://doi.org/10.1002/jclp.22076

Sundman, A. S., Johnsson, M., Wright, D., Jensen, P., & Santos, L. R. (2018). Dogs' ability to follow human communicative cues is not modulated by oxytocin. *Animal Cognition, 21*(3), 405–414. https://doi.org/10.1007/s10071-018-1173-4

Suttie, J. (2020). Overcoming the brain's negativity bias. *Greater Good Science Center.* https://www.dailygood.org/story/2453/overcoming-the-brain-s-negativity-bias-jill-suttie/

Van Edwards, V. (2017). *Captivate: The science of succeeding with people.* Portfolio.

Vedantam, S. (2010). *The hidden brain: How our unconscious minds elect presidents, control markets, wage wars, and save our lives.* Spiegel & Grau.

Vedantam, S., & Mesler, B. (2021). *Useful delusions: The power and paradox of the self-deceiving brain.* W. W. Norton & Company.

Vedantam, S. (Host). (2022, August 1). You 2.0: Befriending your inner voice (with Ethan Kross) [Audio podcast episode]. In *Hidden Brain.* Hidden Brain Media. https://hiddenbrain.org/podcast/you-2-0-befriending-your-inner-voice/

Vedantam, S. (Host). (2022, November 14). Relationships 2.0: An antidote to loneliness (with U.S. Surgeon General Vivek Murthy) [Audio podcast episode]. In *Hidden Brain.* Hidden Brain Media. https://hiddenbrain.org/podcast/relationships-2-0-an-antidote-to-loneliness/

BIBLIOGRAPHY

Vedantam, S. (Host). (2023, January 17). *Persuasion: Part 1 (with Robert Cialdini)* [Audio podcast episode]. In *Hidden Brain*. Hidden Brain Media. https://hiddenbrain.org/podcast/persuasion-part-1/

Vedantam, S. (Host). (2023, February 26). *Happiness 2.0: Surprising Sources of Joy (with Elizabeth Dunn)* [Audio podcast episode]. In *Hidden Brain*. Hidden Brain Media. https://hiddenbrain.org/podcast/happiness-2-0-surprising-sources-of-joy/

Vedantam, S. (Host). (2023, March 6). *Happiness 2.0: The only way out is through (with Todd Kashdan)* [Audio podcast episode]. In *Hidden Brain*. Hidden Brain Media. https://hiddenbrain.org/podcast/happiness-2-0-the-only-way-out-is-through/

Vedantam, S. (Host). (2023, September 4). *Being Kind to Yourself (with Kristin Neff)* [Audio podcast episode]. In *Hidden Brain*. Hidden Brain Media. https://hiddenbrain.org/podcast/being-kind-to-yourself/

Vedantam, S. (Host). (2023, October 2). *Escaping Perfectionism (with Thomas Curran)* [Audio podcast episode]. In *Hidden Brain*. Hidden Brain Media. https://hiddenbrain.org/podcast/how-to-believe-in-yourself/

Vedantam, S. (Host). (2023, December 18). *How to Believe in Yourself (with Adam Grant)* [Audio podcast episode]. In *Hidden Brain*. Hidden Brain Media. https://hiddenbrain.org/podcast/how-to-believe-in-yourself/

Vedantam, S. (Host). (2024, May 13). *Innovation 2.0: The Influence You Have (with Vanessa Bohns)* [Audio podcast episode]. In *Hidden Brain*. Hidden Brain Media. https://hiddenbrain.org/podcast/the-influence-you-have/

Vedantam, S. (Host). (2024, July 3). *How Others See You (with Erica Boothby)* [Audio podcast episode]. In *Hidden Brain*. Hidden Brain Media. https://hiddenbrain.org/podcast/mind-reading-how-others-see-you/

Vedantam, S. (Host). (2024, August 19). *You 2.0: The gift of other people (with Nicholas Epley)* [Audio podcast episode]. In *Hidden Brain*. Hidden Brain Media. https://hiddenbrain.org/podcast/you-2-0-the-gift-of-other-people/

Vedantam, S. (Host). (2024, October 14). *How To Win People Over (with Alison Fragale)* [Audio podcast episode]. In *Hidden Brain*. Hidden Brain Media. https://hiddenbrain.org/podcast/how-to-win-people-over/

Vedantam, S. (Host). (2025, April 14). *Relationships 2.0: The Power of Tiny Interactions + Your Questions Answered: Erica Bailey on Authenticity (with Gillian Sandstrom)* [Audio podcast episode]. In *Hidden Brain*. Hidden Brain Media. https://hiddenbrain.org/podcast/relationships-2-0-the-power-of-tiny-interactions/

Vedantam, S. (Host). (2025, April 21). *Relationships 2.0: Why Did You Do That? + Your Questions Answered: Fred Luskin on Grudges (with Liane Young)* [Audio podcast episode]. In *Hidden Brain*. Hidden Brain Media. https://hiddenbrain.org/podcast/mind-reading-why-did-you-do-that/

Vogel, E. A., Rose, J. P., Roberts, L. R., & Eckles, K. (2014). Social comparison, social media, and self-esteem. *Psychology of Popular Media Culture, 3*(4), 206–222. https://doi.org/10.1037/ppm0000047

Waldinger, R., & Schulz, M. (2023). *The good life: Lessons from the world's longest scientific study of happiness*. Simon and Schuster.

Weissbourd, R., Batanova, M., Lovison, V., & Torres, E. (2021). Combatting the epidemic of loneliness. *Harvard Graduate School of Education*. https://www.gse.harvard.edu/ideas/news/21/02/combatting-epidemic-loneliness

Wheeler, E. A., & Faulkner, M. E. (2015). The "pet effect": Physiological calming in the presence of canines. *Society & Animals, 23*(5), 425–438. https://doi.org/10.1163/15685306-12341374

Zou, X., Tam, K. P., Morris, M. W., Lee, S. L., & Chiu, C. Y. (2009). Culture and self-expression in face-to-face and computer-mediated communication. *Journal of Cross-Cultural Psychology, 40*(3), 284–305. https://doi.org/10.1177/0022022109332845

Take the Next Brave Step

How to Make Friends in College
(Even When It Feels Hard)

College gets lonely fast, but connection is possible. This free college companion guide gives you small, smart ways to make it easier.

✔ Simple ways to start conversations
✔ Relatable student scenarios that show what works
✔ A printable worksheet to take your next brave step

Get your free college companion guide at:
www.sayhellofirst.com

Because you're not behind. You're just getting started.

Let's Stay in Touch

If *Say Hello First* made you feel a little more confident, connected, or understood, I'd love to hear from you.

Whether you want to share a story, ask a question, or leave a review, you can do it all at **www.sayhellofirst.com**.

You'll also find:
- **Monthly connection tips and inspiration**
  (sign up for the newsletter)
- **A place to leave a review** or share your thoughts
- **Updates, tools, and book news**

P.S. If you say hello, I'll do my best to say hello back.

About the Author

Bianca Cummings, LPC, NCC, NPT-C®, is a licensed professional counselor, nationally certified counselor, and certified in neuropsychotherapy. She is based in Fairfield, Connecticut, and helps teens and adults overcome anxiety, build confidence, and form meaningful relationships through integrated, evidence-based approaches to mental wellness.

Bianca holds a B.S. in Psychology from Kennesaw State University and an M.A. in Clinical Mental Health Counseling from Fairfield University. She is a certified trauma therapist and a certified radKIDS instructor—a personal safety and empowerment program for children.

She has worked in both outpatient mental health and private practice settings. Her passion lies in helping people reconnect with themselves and others by building trust, emotional balance, and authentic self-expression.

When she's not working with clients or writing, Bianca enjoys running, hiking, traveling, and exploring the science of human behavior. She's also an avid podcast listener who draws inspiration from conversations about psychology, connection, and personal growth. Most of all, she treasures time spent with her daughter, Stephanie, her partner, Paul, and the lovable puppy she recently adopted, named Friday.

Say Hello First is her debut book and a heartfelt guide to helping people feel less alone, reconnect with their authentic selves, and take the first courageous step toward friendship.

To learn more or reach out, visit www.sayhellofirst.com.